Praise for

Explore the National Marine Sanctuaries with Jean-Michel Cousteau

"This book series gives us deeply felt and profound insight into our country's amazing National Marine Sanctuaries. They are wonderful, illuminating volumes that show the sanctuaries' great beauty and awe. In this critical time of a major oil disaster threatening our natural world, there is an urgent need for the world to learn about these momentous marine sanctuaries and how to protect them. I thank my dear friend, Jean-Michel Cousteau, and Ocean Futures Society, for calling attention to the care of these beautiful marine sanctuaries in our time of extreme need. Jean-Michel is the authoritative servant on the sea for our generation and future generations. This incredible series will be beneficial in getting the word out about the importance of protecting our oceans and the marine life that call it home."

Robert Lyn Nelson
Artist/Environmentalist

"Jean-Michel Cousteau and Ocean Futures Society have set themselves the task of communicating the beauty of the ocean and the necessity of protecting it to the widest possible audience. Through stunning photography and superbly succinct writing, Explore the National Marine Sanctuaries with Jean-Michel Cousteau does just that. This wonderful book series shows how very precious the

USA's National Marine Sanctuaries are, and what a huge contribution the sanctuaries make to our knowledge and understanding of the underwater world. The series is also very timely in light of recent events in the Gulf of Mexico which show how vulnerable the marine environment still is. Oil spillages do not respect marine sanctuaries any more than forest fires respect the boundaries of National Parks.

But without even the protection that the National Marine Sanctuaries offer, America's marine biodiversity—and the public knowledge and appreciation of it—would be the poorer. Those of us whose lives revolve around the protection of wildlife on land, rather than the marine environment, can only admire and envy Jean-Michel's extraordinary success in conserving, communicating and educating. Genuine environmentalists like Jean-Michel know that we need a truly holistic approach to the conservation of wildlife on land and sea. This book series is an undoubted 'treasure-house' and I have no hesitation in recommending it to all who love wildlife and wish to understand better how to redress the terrible imbalance between Man and Nature."

Simon Cowell MBE FRGS MCIJ
Founder, Wildlife Aid; Producer and
Presenter, Wildlife SOS, United Kingdom

"Marine sanctuaries represent the most special places in the ocean. We cannot sustain the ocean without first sustaining our sanctuaries. But like all things in the ocean, they are beneath the surface and invisible to almost everyone. Jean-Michel, through his films and this book series, gives these life and makes the ocean visible and tangible. He is a keen observer of nature and a storyteller about the ocean. He adds a depth of understanding and interpretation that is easy for everyone to grasp."

Daniel J. Basta, Director
NOAA's Office of National Marine Sanctuaries

explore

the West Coast
National Marine Sanctuaries

WITH JEAN-MICHEL COUSTEAU

explore

the West Coast
National Marine Sanctuaries

WITH JEAN-MICHEL COUSTEAU

CHANNEL ISLANDS | MONTEREY BAY | FARALLONES | CORDELL BANK | OLYMPIC COAST

ISBN 978-0-9826940-2-2

Book cover, layout and design by Nate Myers, Wilhelm Design
Editing by Dr. Maia McGuire

Printed in the United States of America

Front Cover: Ocean Futures Team Member Holly Lohuis with Humboldt squid.
           Photo Credit: Carrie Vonderhaar, Ocean Futures Society

10 9 8 7 6 5 4 3 2 1

"Jean-Michel Cousteau and his team have put together an amazing series of books dedicated to the undersea world on which we depend. This is the first time anyone has truly captured the experience of diving America's underwater treasures, the entire national marine sanctuary system. I cannot tell you how truly beautiful and moving a series this is. After spending time with this book, I am even more proud of America's commitment to protect our National Marine Sanctuaries."

Jeff Mora, Los Angeles Lakers executive chef,
board member National Marine Sanctuary Foundation,
International Advisory Board member Ocean Futures Society

"National Marine Sanctuaries are not only extraordinary places to visit, they are also one of our most powerful tools in ocean conservation. Explore the National Marine Sanctuaries with Jean-Michel Cousteau provides an underwater roadmap through the Sanctuaries with compelling stories and magnificent images. For those fortunate enough to have visited Sanctuaries, these books are the perfect way to preserve the memories. For those who have not, they are the next best thing to being there. Most importantly, Explore the National Marine Sanctuaries with Jean-Michel Cousteau teaches us that by protecting National Marine Sanctuaries we help protect the world-ocean...and ourselves."

Bob Talbot Chairman of the Board,
National Marine Sanctuary Foundation;
Board of Directors, Sea Shepherd Conservation Society,
Filmmaker and Photographer

Contents

Foreword

Jean-Michel Cousteau's love of the ocean and the desire to protect it began as a boy, inspired by living on the edge of the Mediterranean Sea and sharing underwater adventures in the Atlantic, Pacific and Indian oceans with his parents, brother, and other pioneering ocean explorers aboard the legendary ship, *Calypso*. Ask him what it is about the ocean that has captured his heart and mind, and he might tell you of face-to-face encounters with curious fish, squid and great white sharks or the joy of gliding through forests of kelp or being underwater at night surrounded by a living cosmos of bioluminescent creatures. He could say how rewarding it is to be an explorer, to be the first to see places and meet forms of life in the sea that have not yet been given names. And, he would likely encourage you to go experience such things for yourself in places such as those celebrated in this volume and others that follow.

Cousteau's deep commitment to the National Marine Sanctuary Program stems from understanding how important the sanctuaries are as a means of protecting the nation's natural, historic and cultural heritage. Like national parks and wildlife management areas on the land, marine sanctuaries safeguard healthy systems and help restore those that have been harmed. While some observers believe the ocean should be able to take care of itself, many species prized for food or sport have declined by 90 percent or more in a few decades. Low oxygen areas, "dead zones," are proliferating, and sea grass meadows and coral reefs are diminishing. Major changes, most not favorable to humankind, are underway, and the sanctuaries can give stressed systems and species a break. We need the oceans, and now the oceans need us to do what it takes to restore health to the world's blue heart.

I share with Jean-Michel Cousteau the delight of being sprayed with whale breath at Stellwagen Bank, dodging sea turtles while looking for fossils of ice age animals at Gray's Reef off the coast of Georgia, of gliding among giant parrotfish in the Florida Keys, and immersing myself in a blizzard of eggs from spawning coral at the Flower Garden Banks off the coasts of Texas and Louisiana. There is haunting beauty and mystery in the protected shipwrecks lying within the Great Lakes, and others such as the remains of the Civil War vessel, *Monitor*, once a home for sailors, now a sanctuary for clouds of small fish and large grouper.

Those who visit any of California's four National Marine Sanctuaries have a chance to glimpse blue whales, the largest animals on earth, as well as some of the smallest, the minute planktonic creatures that drive ocean food webs. The Olympic National Marine Sanctuary holds healthy kelp forests adjacent to stands of ancient trees, and westward, in the Hawaiian Islands, special protection is being provided for some notable annual visitors, humpback whales. Coral reefs and the enormous diversity of life they contain are valued – and protected – in the Northwest Hawaiian Islands, American Samoa and a series of reefs, atolls and deep canyons near the Mariana Islands. These are all vital parts of the nation's treasury, places that give hope for the ocean, and therefore hope for ourselves.

I am pleased to be associated with the Ocean Futures Society, the organization Jean-Michel Cousteau founded to explore, communicate discoveries and messages to people and inspire them to take action to restore and protect the living ocean. They are making a difference – and so can you. Your reading of this book series is a strong first step in your understanding of the importance of protecting the sanctuaries for generations to come.

Dr. Sylvia Earle
Oakland, California

Preface

The National Marine Sanctuary sites were designated in part because they were imperiled. Created more than 100 years after the national park system, these underwater treasures have been more difficult to explore and we have worked hard to learn their true value. By the time we did, we also discovered they were already at risk. Their very existence speaks to a changing reality that we now understand. It is clear that sanctuaries protect and promote the abundance and diversity of marine life essential to a healthy ocean, and I am gratified that our leaders have made it a priority to protect them now and for the future.

Welcome to the *National Marine Sanctuaries on the West Coast of the United States.* In this book, my dive team and I introduce you to the incredibly beautiful natural world of five marine sanctuaries established by the National Oceanic and Atmospheric Administration.

The National Marine Sanctuaries featured in this book are very special to me and my Ocean Futures Society Team. Our headquarters is located in Santa Barbara, California, in the heart of the Channel Islands National Marine Sanctuary. We have had the great pleasure of exploring the Sanctuary's many natural wonders, on land and under water. We have a special connection with Santuary staff members and are amazed at the great natural beauty we discover on our frequent trips throughout the Sanctuary's islands. In addition to the Sanctuary's natural wonders, we have been fascinated by the historical connection with the Chumash people, whose ancestors survived living from the land and from the bounty of the surrounding sea. Also protected as the Channel Islands National Park, these islands and surrounding marine environment are considered the North Galapagos with a rich diversity of species; a true Amecian treasure.

North along the California coast are three more sanctuaries, each with different natural wonders. The largest is the Monterey Bay National Marine Sanctuary, which is not only the largest but is also one of the most spectacular. Monterey Bay offers visitors easy access to observe the diverse marine life found there, from the smallest sea creatures to the largest mammals in the world. Like the Channel Islands, Monterey Bay has many charter boat operators who are licensed to introduce visitors via boat trips offshore as well as an innovative aquarium for those who want to stay on shore and still experience the uniqueness of this underwater haven.

While both the Gulf of the Farallones and Cordell Bank National Marine Sanctuaries are more difficult to visit, they are exceptional examples of the undersea world found off the coast of San Francisco. Many fish species and other marine life make these sanctuaries perfect locations for scientific research and for visitors seeking a better understanding of the ocean world. In diving these sanctuaries, we were more physically challenged than at any of the other sanctuaries because of the deep water, strong and changing currents, and large marine species.

The Olympic Coast National Marine Sanctuary, the farthest north of the sanctuaries, is situated on the west coast of Washington State. This area is home to the Makah people, whose lives and traditions are linked with the ocean and coastal lands through centuries of time.

I hope that you enjoy your journey through the Sanctuaries in this book, and that you will visit them to see their wonders for yourself. Every American now has the opportunity to experience these underwater treasures that are protected for all generations and especially for the future.

I invite you to read the three other books in the series *Explore the National Marine Sanctuaries with Jean-Michel Cousteau* which take you to the sanctuaries in the Southeast, Northeast and Pacific Islands.

Jean-Michel Cousteau
Santa Barbara, California

Introduction

About this Series

The four-book series, *Explore the National Marine Sanctuaries with Jean-Michel Cousteau*, has been developed in partnership with the National Marine Sanctuary system and Ocean Futures Society. Text in *italics* is excerpted from the previously-published (2007), limited-edition book *America's Underwater Treasures* by Jean-Michel Cousteau and Julie Robinson with photography by Carrie Vonderhaar. That book describes the experience and research of Jean-Michel and his Ocean Futures Team while diving all 13 underwater marine sanctuaries and the one underwater marine monument. Their experiences are captured in a film by the same name aired on PBS as part of *Jean-Michel Cousteau's Ocean Adventures*. The current series is offered to make information on these vital sanctuaries even more inclusive for the American public.

Each book in the series takes readers to one of the four regions of the country into which NOAA has organized its management of the National Marine Sanctuaries. This book, *Explore the West Coast National Marine Sanctuaries with Jean-Michel Cousteau*, visits sanctuaries off the coast of California and Washington. The other books in the series are: *Explore the Southeast National Marine Sanctuaries with Jean-Michel Cousteau, Explore the Northeast National Marine Sanctuaries with Jean-Michel Cousteau and Explore the Pacific Islands National Marine Sanctuaries with Jean-Michel Cousteau.*

Jean-Michel Cousteau.
Photo credit: Matthew Ferraro, Ocean Futures Society.

The first National Marine Sanctuary in the United States was established only three decades ago, while Yellowstone, the oldest of America's National Parks, was created in 1872. By comparison to parks, these natural marine jewels were damaged upon arrival. Only small portions remain pristine. For many, their designations arose amidst threats to one or a number of aspects to their survival. Like terrestrial parks, these are special habitats, managed zones for the recovery of critical species like humpback whales or juvenile rockfish but, most importantly, they attempt to preserve the integrity of the web of life.

Ironically, we discovered that managing these resources for sustainability was in truth an exercise in managing ourselves. And that's not, as we're still learning, an easy job. At each destination we were privileged witnesses to the real-time drama of marine conservation playing out across the United States. At the heart of it all, we found a powerful paradigm shift happening in environmentalism. Fishermen, environmentalists and scientists from opposite sides of the aisle were sitting down together with rolled-up sleeves, poring through scientific research, debating the merits of reserves and restoration, and coming to terms with this new definition of sanctuary. "These are," as Dan Basta, Director of the National Marine Sanctuary System, reminded us, "still works in progress."

About National Marine Sanctuaries

The Office of National Marine Sanctuaries, part of the National Oceanic and Atmospheric Administration, manages a national system of underwater-protected areas. The National Marine Sanctuary Act (created in 1972) authorizes the Secretary of Commerce to designate specific areas as National Marine Sanctuaries to promote comprehensive management of their special ecological, historical, recreational, and aesthetic resources. The Office of National Marine Sanctuaries currently manages thirteen National Marine Sanctuaries and one Marine National Monument established in areas where the natural or cultural resources are so significant that they warrant special status and protection.

On January 6, 2009, President George W. Bush established three additional marine national monuments, which were placed into the Pacific Reefs National Wildlife Refuge Complex. The three new marine national monuments are the Pacific Remote Islands Marine National Monument, Marianas Trench Marine National Monument, and the Rose Atoll Marine National Monument. Because Jean-Michel Cousteau and his Ocean Futures Society team have not yet dived in these three remote areas, they are not included in this series. Furthermore, these new monuments are managed by the US Fish and Wildlife Service, and not by the National Oceanic and Atmospheric Administration, the managing agency of the National Marine Sanctuaries and one Marine National Monument featured here.

The Office of National Marine Sanctuaries works cooperatively with the public and federal, state, and local officials to promote conservation while allowing compatible commercial and recreational activities in the Sanctuaries. Increasing public awareness of our marine heritage, scientific research, monitoring, exploration, educational programs, and outreach are just a few of the ways the Office of National Marine Sanctuaries fulfills its mission to the American people. The primary objective of a sanctuary is to protect its natural and cultural features while allowing people to use and enjoy the ocean in a sustainable way. Sanctuary waters provide a secure habitat for species close to extinction and protect historically significant shipwrecks and artifacts. Sanctuaries serve as natural classrooms and laboratories for schoolchildren and researchers alike to promote understanding and stewardship of our oceans. They often are cherished recreational spots for sport fishing and diving and support commercial industries such as tourism, fishing and kelp harvesting.

Today (2007), only 0.01 percent of the world's oceans are effectively protected, a comparatively small measure, and one most scientists are quick to caution isn't a panacea for all the ocean's troubles. But it's enough nonetheless, to keep some fisheries managers and fishermen hopeful about sustainably harvesting fish from the sea. In the face of collapsing fisheries, "They may help some exploited species recover and keep others from going entirely extinct," according to Daniel Pauly, a researcher with the Fisheries Center at the University of British Columbia. He postulates that marine protected areas "should help prevent this, just like forests and other natural terrestrial habitats have enabled the survival of wildlife species, which agriculture would have otherwise rendered extinct."

The mission of NOAA's National Marine Sanctuaries is to serve as the trustee for the nation's system of marine protected areas, to conserve, protect, and enhance their biodiversity, ecological integrity and cultural legacy. The National Marine Sanctuary System consists of more than 150,000 square miles (390,000 km²) of marine and Great Lakes waters located from Washington State to the Florida Keys; from Lake Huron to American Samoa. Within these protected waters, giant humpback whales breed and calve their young, temperate reefs flourish, and shipwrecks tell stories of our maritime history. Today, our marine sanctuary system encompasses deep ocean gardens, nearshore coral reefs, whale migration corridors, deep sea canyons, and even underwater archeological sites. The sites range in size from one-quarter square mile (0.6 km²) in Fagatele Bay, American Samoa to more than 135,000 square miles (350,000 km²) in the Northwestern Hawaiian Islands, one of the largest marine protected areas in the world. Each sanctuary site is a unique place needing special protections. Natural classrooms, cherished recreational spots, and valuable commercial industries—marine sanctuaries represent many things to many people.

The National Marine Sanctuaries' West Coast Region

The five West Coast national marine sanctuaries encompass 12,682 square miles (32,846 km²) of ocean, including hundreds of miles of dramatic coastline. Teeming with life and filled with history, they offer countless opportunities for exploration, recreation and contemplation. The West Coast Region seeks to support research into human connections to the sea that include indigenous native cultures, seafaring traditions and the discovery and protection of maritime heritage resources, such as shipwrecks, and those objects which remain in place to remind us of historic activities including lighthouses, historic wharves, docks and piers. The West Coast Regional office of the national marine sanctuaries manages marine protected areas around the **Channel Islands**, **Monterey Bay, Gulf of the Farallones**, **Cordell Bank** and **Olympic Coast**. Each of the five West Coast national marine sanctuaries is a jewel unto itself. Yet each of these sanctuaries is intimately connected not only with the others, but also to the entire coast from Alaska to Baja California, Mexico and to the far reaches of the world ocean via ocean currents.

West Coast Regional Office:
99 Pacific Street, Bldg. 200, Suite K
Monterey, CA 93940
Telephone: 831-647-1920
Fax: 831-647-1732

Overlapping Themes in the Five West Coast National Marine Sanctuaries

Each of these five sanctuaries is a special place with its own unique character. Each has a distinct set of physical conditions, including climate, daily weather patterns, the lay of the coast and the make-up of the seafloor. These and other factors help define the nature of each sanctuary and set each apart from the others. However, in the restless ocean, driven by wind and storms and powerful currents, no place is truly isolated from any other.

CALIFORNIA CURRENT/ UPWELLING

The national marine sanctuaries on the West Coast are linked by the California Current—a broad, shallow "river" of ocean water meandering southward along the Pacific Coast. This slow-moving surface current carries some 10 trillion gallons (38 trillion liters) of water per hour—a flow 55 times greater than the Amazon River. Carrying cold, nutrient-rich water southward from the North Pacific, the California Current shapes the nature of the entire West Coast, setting the stage for an abundance and diversity of ocean life equaled in only a few other places on Earth. Below it, two counter currents, the Davidson Current and the deeper California Undercurrent, flow north.

Kayaking off the Channel Islands. Photo credit: Claire Fackler, NOAA National Marine Sanctuaries.

Seabirds dive on a ball of schooling fish in front of Anacapa Island, part of the Channel Islands National Marine Sanctuary. Photo credit: Carrie Vonderhaar, Ocean Futures Society.

When it runs strong, the current carries drifting plants and animals southward from sub-arctic waters. When it slackens in the fall, the surface waters warm and southern species move northward. This ever-shifting mix of species adds to the great diversity of marine communities in the West Coast National Marine Sanctuaries. The current serves as a vast, open highway for whales, birds, fishes and plankton, which follow it on long migrations in search of food or suitable places to nest, spawn or give birth. For some—such as Pacific sardines, northern anchovies, gray whales, Western Gulls and Brandt's Cormorants—the boundaries of their lives are largely defined by the boundaries of the California Current.

This moment of birth shows an elephant seal with her newborn pup, visible in the sac still attached to the mother. Photo credit: Carrie Vonderhaar, Ocean Futures Society.

Vast schools of sardines, anchovies and hake spawn in the warmer waters around the Channel Islands, then swim north through the other sanctuaries where they find rich pastures of plankton to feed on. The small fishes are joined by giant blue whales and other whales that come to feed on krill and other plankton. Salmon spawned in streams along the Olympic Coast follow the current north to the Gulf of Alaska and south to Cordell Bank, Gulf of the Farallones, Monterey Bay and the Channel Islands sanctuaries in search of food. Gray whales traverse the entire coast, passing through all five sanctuaries twice each year as they migrate from Alaska to Baja California, Mexico. Meanwhile, pods of transient prowl the coastal waters of Monterey Bay and the Santa Barbara Channel in spring to hunt gray whale calves as they swim north with their mothers. Elephant seals, sea lions and fur seals roam widely along the coast and far out to sea, then return to rookeries in the Channel Islands, Monterey Bay and the Gulf of the Farallones sanctuaries where they give birth to their pups.

Black-footed albatross. Photo credit: Josh Pederson, Monterey Bay National Marine Sanctuary.

A brown pelican or black storm petrel appearing along the Olympic Coast may have been hatched and fledged on the Channel Islands. Some 400,000 gulls, cormorants and murres nest in the Gulf of the Farallones, and then fly far and wide to the other sanctuaries and beyond. These sanctuaries protect vital habitat for shorebirds and countless species along the important migration route known as the Pacific Flyway.

The connections extend further still as other species pass through these waters on their way to and from more distant places. Each year, albacore tuna follow currents across the Pacific Ocean and back again; sooty shearwaters travel here from as far away as New Zealand; and leatherback turtles migrate from Indonesia. Albatrosses breeding on the Northwestern Hawaiian Islands regularly fly back and forth to the Olympic Coast and Northern California National Marine Sanctuaries to find food for their chicks.

The productive ecosystem off the coast of California has three oceanographic seasons: upwelling season in the spring and early summer, relaxation in the late summer and fall, and the storm season in winter.

Upwelling Season: During the upwelling season (March to July), strong northwest winds and the south-flowing California Current combine with the earth's rotation to drive surface waters away from the shore. These surface waters are replaced by an upwelling of nutrient-rich deeper water from offshore. The nutrients become available for surface dwelling phytoplankton (microscopic marine algae). Phytoplankton form the foundation of this oceanic food web and the combination of nutrients and increased sunlight in spring initiates a bloom of life that radiates up the food web. An abundance of phytoplankton, zooplankton, and young fish are food for animals at higher levels of the marine food web.

A student closely examines a water sample after a plankton tow in the Channel Islands National Marine Sanctuary. Photo credit: Claire Fackler, NOAA National Marine Sanctuaries.

Rocks at Pescadero State Beach, just south of Half Moon Bay, California are pounded by a winter swell. Photo credit: Carrie Vonderhaar, Ocean Futures Society.

Relaxation Season/Oceanic Period: During the late summer and fall (August to early November), coastal winds weaken and the sea surface becomes calmer. Surface currents during this time period are mostly northward and water temperatures increase. During this time, coastal waters are rich with the products of upwelling, and many migratory animals are in the area feeding on an abundance of prey.

Winter Storm Season/Davidson Current Period: The winter storm season (mid-November through February) is dominated by rough seas and greater mixing of ocean water. Strong winter storms originating in the Gulf of Alaska cause turbulent conditions that mix the stratified ocean layers in the upper water column. This results in similar temperature, salinity, and concentration of nutrients throughout the water column.

School of sardines in a kelp forest off Anacapa Island, Channel Islands National Marine Sanctuary and National Park. Photo credit: Robert Schwemmer, NOAA National Marine Sanctuaries.

KELP FORESTS

Kelp forests grow predominantly on the Pacific Coast, from Alaska and Canada to the waters of Baja California, Mexico. Tiered like a terrestrial rainforest with a canopy and several layers below, the kelp forests of the eastern Pacific coast are dominated by two canopy-forming, brown macroalgae species, giant kelp and bull kelp. Native Americans used kelp as a source of medicine, food, salt, and fishing gear. Modern day uses include the extraction of algin, which is used in everyday products, such as paints, pharmaceuticals, rubber, beer and toothpaste.

Four national marine sanctuaries harbor kelp forests. Giant kelp is found in the Channel Islands National Marine Sanctuary. Giant kelp and bull kelp coexist in the Monterey Bay National Marine Sanctuary. In the more northern Gulf of the Farallones and Olympic Coast National Marine Sanctuaries, kelp forests are comprised of predominantly bull kelp.

It's a little strange, from a terrestrial point of view, to learn that the fastest growing plant on Earth is actually found in the sea. The formidable seaweed Macrocystis pyrifera, the giant kelp, can grow up to two feet (60 cm) a day under ideal conditions and reaches nearly 200 feet (6 meters). Along the coast of California, giant kelp is the tree of life, the supporting foundation of the nearshore marine ecosystem. At least eighty species of plants, fish and invertebrates depend entirely upon kelp for food and shelter; almost one thousand forms of life use it at least part of the time. While the similarities are only superficial, leaf-like blades, stem-like stipes and root-like holdfasts mimic the structure of terrestrial trees. Without the roots of a true vascular plant, these swaying forests absorb nutrients straight from the sea, relying on sunlight for photosynthesis and clear, clean water to thrive and grow. Though they tower above the seafloor, these algae reside on the lower rung of the food web. Herbivores like urchins, abalone and turban or jewel-topped snails graze on kelp. And when predators like southern sea otters, spiny lobsters and sheephead are absent, urchins in particular can quickly deforest the marinescape. Warm temperatures during El Niño and heavy nutrients that reduce light during La Niña, as well as decadal ocean cycles and coastal pollution can all have negative impacts, causing ripples to spread up the trophic levels, eventually impacting seals, sea lions, and fish stocks which consequently can cause dramatic economic impacts for us.

A garibaldi, California's state fish, patrols the kelp forest.
Photo credit: Carrie Vonderhaar, Ocean Futures Society.

Bull kelp. Photo credit: Josh Pederson, Monterey Bay National Marine Sanctuary.

Kelp forests grow along rocky coastlines in depths of about six feet to more than 90 feet (two meters to 30 m). Kelp favors nutrient-rich, cool waters that range in temperature from 42° to 72°F (5° to 20°C). These brown algae communities live in clear water conditions through which light penetrates easily. Kelp recruits most successfully in regions of upwelling (regions where the ocean layers overturn, bringing cool, nutrient-rich bottom waters to the surface) and regions with continuously cold, high-nutrient waters. Kelp experiences reduced or negative growth rates in warm water. This phenomenon is particularly evident in southern California where giant kelp forests deteriorate in the summer months. Along the central California coast, where the distribution of giant kelp and bull kelp overlap, giant kelp out-competes bull kelp for light.

Uprooted giant kelp holdfast in the Channel Islands National Marine Sanctuary.
Photo credit: Claire Fackler, NOAA National Marine Sanctuaries.

Instead of tree-like roots that extend into the substrate, kelp has "anchors" called holdfasts that grip onto rocky substrates. From the holdfasts, kelp plants grow toward the water's surface. Gas bladders called pneumatocysts keep the upper portions of the algae afloat. A giant kelp plant has a pneumatocyst at the base of each blade. In contrast, a bull kelp plant has only one pneumatocyst that supports several blades near the water's surface. Kelp survival is positively correlated with the strength of the substrate. The larger and stronger the rock on which it is anchored, the greater the chance of kelp survival. Winter storms and high-energy environments easily uproot the kelp and can wash entire plants ashore.

Purple urchins devour a kelp holdfast. In areas where urchin predator populations have been decimated little to no kelp can be found, creating what are called urchin barrens. Photo credit: Carrie Vonderhaar, Ocean Futures Society.

The kelp forests in Gulf of the Farallones National Marine Sanctuary are small and localized compared to those in the Channel Islands, Monterey Bay, and Olympic Coast sanctuaries. Kelp forest development in Gulf of the Farallones National Marine Sanctuary may be hampered by high-energy waves, lack of suitable substrate, predation on young kelp plants by sea urchins, and high turbidity and variations in salinity caused by water flowing out from San Francisco Bay.

Giant kelp is a perennial (it can live for up to seven years) while bull kelp is an annual (it completes its life cycle in one year). Both types of kelp have a two-stage life cycle. They exist in their earliest life stages as spores, released with millions of others from the parent kelp. The spores grow into a tiny male or female plant called a gametophyte, which produces either sperm or eggs. After fertilization occurs, the embry-

Giant kelp off Santa Barbara Island in the Channel Islands National Marine Sanctuary.
Photo credit: Richard Murphy, Ocean Futures Society.

os may grow into mature plants, completing the life cycle. Giant kelp has an average growth (in spring) of 10 inches (27 cm) per day, yet it may grow up to two feet (60 cm) per day. By contrast, the average growth of bull kelp is about four inches (10 cm) per day.

A host of invertebrates, fish, marine mammals, and birds exist in kelp forest environs. From the holdfasts to the surface mats of kelp fronds, the array of habitats on the kelp itself may support thousands of invertebrate individuals. California sea lions, harbor seals, sea otters, and whales may feed in the kelp or escape storms or predators in the shelter of kelp. On rare occasions gray whales have been spotted seeking refuge in kelp forests from predatory killer whales. All larger marine life, including birds and mammals, may retreat to kelp during storm events because the kelp helps to weaken currents and waves.

This north-bound migrating gray whale hugs the shoreline of the Olympic Coast National Marine Sanctuary. Photo credit: Carrie Vonderhaar, Ocean Futures Society.

Perhaps the most familiar image of kelp forests is a picture of a sea otter draped in strands of kelp, gripping a sea urchin on its belly. Both sea otters and sea urchins play critical roles in the stable equilibrium ecosystem. Sea urchins graze kelp and may reach population densities large enough to destroy kelp forests at the rate of 30 feet (9 meters) per month. Urchins move in "herds," and enough urchins may remain in the "barrens" of a former kelp forest to negate any attempt at regrowth. Sea otters, playing a critical role in containing the urchin populations, prey on urchins and thus control the numbers of kelp grazers.

Southern sea otters are an important species in a kelp forest. A well-balanced ecosystem will have enough sea otters to keep sea floor herbivores, like urchins, in check. Photo credit: Carrie Vonderhaar, Ocean Futures Society.

When present in healthy numbers, sea otters keep sea urchin populations in check. But when sea otters decline, urchin numbers explode and grab onto kelp like flies on honey. The urchins chew off the anchors that keep the kelp in place, causing them to die and float away, setting off a chain reaction that depletes the food supply for other marine animals causing their numbers to decline.

By the early 20th century, when sea otters were nearly hunted out of existence for their fur, kelp beds disappeared and so did the marine life that depended on kelp. Years later, conservationists moved some remaining otters from Big Sur to Central California. Gradually, their numbers grew, sea urchin numbers declined, and the kelp began to grow again. As the underwater forests grew, other species reappeared.

A plethora of California sea lions diving in a kelp forest off San Miguel Island in the Channel Islands National Marine Sanctuary. Photo credit: Claire Fackler, NOAA National Marine Sanctuaries.

10 Steps To Better Eco-Diving In Kelp Forests
BY JEAN-MICHEL COUSTEAU

The kelp forest is a unique and diversified ecosystem that will provide you with many hours of interesting dives. Since the potential exists for divers to become entangled in kelp it is important to practice safe diving techniques, both to protect the diver and to avoid damaging the kelp plants. Streamlining one's equipment, navigating under the kelp canopy and making proper descents and ascents will make kelp diving enjoyable and safe. Divers should try practicing the exercises below with a buddy:

Step 1—Become comfortable in the water.

Learn the basic skills of diving well enough to be completely at ease. You'll be safer, enjoy more of what you're seeing and be less prone to panic.

Step 2—Plan your dive well.

Dive planning is a cornerstone of basic diving technique, not just the skill of experienced divers. Know the unique characteristics of a dive site in advance so that you do not become disoriented, or even lost. If currents or visibility change unexpectedly, you may be swept onto a reef or into kelp, injuring yourself and marine life if you are not prepared.

Step 3—Learn to control your buoyancy.

Mastering the art of buoyancy control means your dives will be less strenuous and less environmentally damaging. You'll have more time and air to enjoy the underwater scenery.

Step 4—Streamline your equipment.

All equipment should be streamlined so the kelp has as few points as possible to snag on. Once all straps are adjusted, excess material can be trimmed, cut, taped or in some cases reversed, so the excess is on the inside and not flapping around. Keeping gear to a minimum and close to your body also reduces the effort of diving.

Step 5—Learn how to descend and ascend in the kelp.

If you are in the kelp canopy and need to descend, deflate your BC and dry suit (if wearing one) and slowly make a couple of 360 degree turns while your hands push the kelp away. This will make an open area in the kelp. When you descend, lift your arms up over your head, turn, and swim. Similarly, if you need to ascend through the kelp canopy, make a slow ascent while turning 360 degrees and pushing the kelp away, creating an open area at the surface.

Step 6—Swim below the kelp canopy at the surface, navigating with your compass.
If you accidentally surface within the canopy and need to swim across the kelp, extend both of your arms over the kelp in front of you and push the kelp down carefully while doing a dolphin kick. This will pop you up and over the kelp and allow you to move slowly across and out of the canopy.

Step 7—Do not thrash around or make sudden movements if entangled in kelp.
This will only make your situation worse. Reach around or over yourself and remove the kelp. Have your buddy assist with gently untangling the kelp. If you are in an emergency situation, remain calm, find where you are connected to the kelp and bend the kelp back, like snapping a twig, in order to break free.

Step 8—Touch or take nothing.
Your slightest touch can disturb or destroy many residents of the kelp ecosystem. Kelp forests are finely tuned ecosystems inhabited by creatures performing many services that keep the ecosystem functioning. Removing even the most insignificant-appearing stone can disrupt this fragile system. You're a guest in this ocean home. Respect it as you would your own.

Step 9—Think about what your photo or video can do to help the oceans.
Whenever you dive, you impact the undersea environment, and when you take photos or video footage, you bring away a piece of the spirit of the sea. Make your picture as important to the sea as it is to you. You can do this by sharing your experiences with others and by explaining to people how the kelp bed ecosystem functions. If your photos or video are good enough you may want to make presentations to local schools or community service organizations.

Step 10—Be an ambassador of the environment.
Divers are a privileged minority who know the glory of the undersea world. In addition to communicating the beauty and wonder of the kelp bed, use your position and knowledge to promote responsible management of these valuable ecosystems. Support local marine protected areas and our National Marine Sanctuaries.

Fabien Cousteau explores the wreck of the Peacock, the sister ship to his grandfather's legendary vessel, Calypso. Photo credit: Carrie Vonderhaar, Ocean Futures Society.

MARITIME HERITAGE RESOURCES

The national marine sanctuaries on the West Coast share a long and diverse maritime history. They hold remnants of that history in the hundreds of ships that lie wrecked in their waters. These historic maritime heritage resources preserve a seafaring legacy dating back to early explorers, traders, whalers, fishermen and immigrants who have traveled this coast since the mid-1500s.

For hundreds of years, mariners transiting this region along the West Coast of North America have been faced with prevailing winds, extreme weather conditions and natural hazards. Early maritime activities resulted in many ships running aground or sinking within the dangerous cold waters, leaving us today with hundreds of historic shipwrecks, some recorded[1] and many still to be discovered. These wrecks reveal the diverse range of activities and nationalities that traversed the coastal maritime trade routes and are time-capsules of our Nation's seafaring past. They include vessels engaged in various trades such as the California Gold Rush, passenger and cargo, lumber, international coal and grain, fisheries, military, and island commerce, to name a few.

Fierce storms and a rocky shoreline have combined to make the Olympic Coast National Marine Sanctuary a graveyard for ships. Historic records reveal that more than 200 ship-wrecks have been documented in the sanctuary. Many simply disappeared, their epithet written by the lighthouse keeper at Tatoosh, "Last sighted, Cape Flattery."

Cordell Bank was discovered by accident in 1853 when hydrographer George Davidson was returning to San Francisco from a mapping expedition in northern California. In 1869, Edward Cordell, of the U.S. Coast Survey, officially surveyed the area that now bears his name. Cordell Bank National Marine Sanctuary is the sole West Coast sanctuary without any known heritage sites. The sanctuary's deep waters and distance from shore make it less likely for ships to run aground there.

---

1   http://channelislands.noaa.gov/shipwreck/shiphome.html

Pilot seat of Avenger wreck as seen from above. Photo credit: Robert Schwemmer, NOAA Channel Islands National Marine Sanctuary.

Powerful storms, thick fog and strong currents have claimed nearly 200 ships in the waters of Gulf of the Farallones National Marine Sanctuary. The earliest recorded shipwreck was the Spanish Manila galleon *San Agustin*, which sank in a gale while anchored in Drake's Bay in 1595. More recently, the freighter *Jacob Luckenbach* went down 17 miles (27 km) off the Golden Gate Bridge in 1953 after colliding with the steamship *Hawaiian Pilot*. Over the next few decades it was the source of a number of "mystery" oil spills. The NOAA Maritime Heritage Program determined through historical research that the ship was a likely source of the oil discharges. Those suspicions were confirmed through the combined efforts of the local sport diving community, who investigated the site, and the sanctuary's BeachWatch volunteer monitoring program. In 2002, the sanctuary, working with

Freighter CHICKASAW stranded in 1962 off Santa Rosa Island, Channel Islands National Marine Sanctuary. Photo credit: Robert Schwemmer, NOAA National Marine Sanctuaries.

the U.S. Coast Guard and other agencies, took part in an effort to pump approximately 100,000 gallons (378,500 liters) of oil from the wreck's deep bunker tanks, ending the mystery oil spills.

Monterey Bay and the surrounding coast were long a center of trade and a base for fishing and whaling. Nearly 400 ships have been recorded as lost in this region, the largest sanctuary along the West Coast. One tragic event occurred in 1929 when the oil tanker *S.C.T. Dodd* rammed the passenger steamer *San Juan* off Pigeon Point, sending 73 passengers and crewmen to their deaths. The submerged remains of the rigid airship USS *Macon* and four

Port wing of one of four Curtiss Sparrowhawk F9C-2 biplanes found at the USS Macon site. Photo credit: NOAA/MBARI.

Curtiss F9C-2 "Sparrowhawk" aircraft lie off Point Sur, California. The site was first recorded in the 1990s by the U.S. Navy, working in partnership with the Monterey Bay Aquarium Research Institute. In 2006, the sanctuary led an expedition to conduct the first archaeological survey of the site. On February 12, 2010, commemorating the 75th anniversary of the sinking of the airship, the Monterey Bay National Marine Sanctuary announced the USS *Macon* listing on the National Register of Historic Places.

More than 150 historic ships and military aircraft have been lost at the Channel Islands. Each has a story to tell about the history, technology and society of earlier times. Today, NOAA, Channel Islands National Park and the Coastal Maritime Archaeology Resources group record the archaeological remains of the maritime heritage sites on and around the Channel Islands. Exhibits featuring some of the shipwrecks in the sanctuary are on display at the Santa Barbara Maritime Museum. As of 2011, a total of 75 heritage sites have been discovered and documented in the west coast region.

Paddle wheel shaft of Winfield Scott wreck. Photo credit: Robert Schwemmer, NOAA Channel Islands National Marine Sanctuary.

To learn more about maritime heritage resources within the National Marine Sanctuary System visit the National Maritime Heritage Program's website.[2]

2　http://sanctuaries.noaa.gov/maritime/

MBARI's M2 mooring. The sensors on this buoy collect various oceanographic and atmospheric measurements around the clock. Photo credit: Matthew Ferraro, Ocean Futures Society.

OCEAN OBSERVING SYSTEM

The West Coast Observations Network is comprised of 36 instrumented mooring arrays located at long term monitoring or sentinel sites within the five sanctuaries. The moorings collect information on ocean temperature at multiple depths. In certain locations, data about current speed and direction, oxygen, salinity, turbidity, and fluorescence, along with meteorological information, are also collected.

In addition to fixed moorings, the sanctuary program's sister vessels R/V Fulmar and R/V Shearwater, collect and transmit oceanographic and meteorological data in near real time. An online interactive map[3] shows the latest vessel locations and recent data reports.

---

3   http://www.ncddc.noaa.gov/website/google_maps/PaCOOS/mapsPaCOOS.htm

The NOAA research vessel Shearwater working in the waters of the Channel Islands National Marine Sanctuary. Photo credit: Carrie Vonderhaar, Ocean Futures Society.

The information from these platforms is archived and fed into the NOAA-wide Pacific Coastal Ocean Observing Systems project. The data will help resource managers, including the sanctuary program, in the western North Pacific region to better understand the physical, chemical and biological processes in the region. This information can be useful when responding to incidents such as oil spills or accidents at sea, in following impacts of stormwater runoff, and in trying to predict population trends for marine animals.

Channel Islands National Marine Sanctuary

About the Channel Islands National Marine Sanctuary

Just 60 miles (96 km) away but a world apart from Los Angeles, five of eight Channel Islands—Anacapa, Santa Cruz, Santa Rosa, San Miguel and Santa Barbara—are encircled within a protective boundary. And through a unique caretaking partnership, the National Park Service and National Marine Sanctuary Program are working together to address the needs of the marine and terrestrial ecosystems.

Twenty-five miles (40 km) off the coast of Santa Barbara, the waters around the Channel Islands host an incredible array of marine life and habitats. Here, warm and cold water currents collide to create a transition zone where cold water species blend with warmer water species to create unique and diverse marine communities.

Channel Islands National Marine Sanctuary and Channel Islands National Park were both designated in 1980 to protect these communities and to preserve cultural and archeological treasures. The nation's third sanctuary encompasses 1,470 square miles (3,800 km²) of ocean around Anacapa, Santa Cruz, Santa Rosa, San Miguel and Santa Barbara Islands. The sanctuary sits amid some of California's richest fishing grounds. To help protect and restore this fragile ecosystem, 11 marine reserves closed to all fishing and two state marine conservation areas open to limited fishing, have been set aside.

Channel Islands. Photo credit: Claire Fackler, NOAA National Marine Sanctuaries.

Waves crashing into Santa Rosa Island. Photo credit: Claire Fackler, NOAA National Marine Sanctuaries.

Experimental, bold and not without conflict, the…expansion of the Channel Islands marine reserve network aims at nothing short of saving what remains, and restoring balance to an ecosystem cart-wheeling towards collapse. At its heart is a simple premise for recovery: juveniles need to grow up and reproduce. But the piecemeal approach of regulating species while ignoring the larger ecosystem hasn't worked. The logical alternative is an "ecosystem-based management" approach, considering all species, even ones we do not harvest, because all species are connected in the intricate web of life of a healthy ecosystem.

Between them, these protected areas cover 318 square miles (823 km²). The national park also protects the five islands and their surrounding waters out to one nautical mile (1.1 mile/1.8 km). Visitors to the islands can walk along sandy beaches and rocky shores studded with tide pools. Seagrass meadows thrive in shallow, soft-bottomed areas. Giant kelp form dense underwater forests of amber and gold that attract sport divers from around the world.

More than 30 species of marine mammals, including gray, blue, and humpback whales, come to feast on the bounty, as do more than 60 species of sea birds. The Channel Islands National Marine Sanctuary currently provides habitat for breeding populations of four species of pinnipeds: the California sea lion, the northern fur seal, the northern elephant seal, and the harbor seal. Stellar sea lions and Guadalupe fur seals are rare visitors to the area. All six species are found in the sanctuary at different times of year, feeding on abundant fish and invertebrate resources of the island shelves or hauling out on rocks and beaches. The islands provide important nesting sites for black storm petrels and Xantus's murrelets. Anacapa Island is the only permanent rookery in California for threatened California brown pelicans. More than 60 species of birds feed in the sanctuary and more than 23 species of sharks occur here.

The islands are also rich in history. Archaeologists have found remnants of sites occupied by the early Chumash peoples dating back thousands of years. The prevailing currents and weather conditions made shipwrecks a common occurrence here; more than 150 aircraft and shipwrecks lie on the seafloor around the Islands.

Giant kelp in the Channel Islands National Marine Sanctuary. Photo credit: Claire Fackler, NOAA National Marine Sanctuaries.

California brown pelican. Photo credit: Carrie Vonderhaar, Ocean Futures Society.

Why a National Marine Sanctuary?

The Channel Islands have long served as a resource for humans. The Chumash were the first people to inhabit the Channel Islands. The islands were first visited by Europeans in 1542. In the 1800s the islands served as a location for sea otter, seal, and sea lion hunting. Subsequently, the land was cultivated for ranching and farming purposes. Located offshore of Southern California, the sanctuary is adjacent to the growing counties of Ventura and Santa Barbara, and not far from the heavily populated Los Angeles metropolitan area.

California sea lions are famous for their curiosity about divers. Photo credit: Carrie Vonderhaar, Ocean Futures Society.

Federal efforts to protect the islands began in 1938 when President Franklin D. Roosevelt proclaimed Santa Barbara and Anacapa islands as the Channel Islands National Monument. In 1976, a U.S. Navy and National Park Service agreement allowed supervised visitation of San Miguel Island. In 1978, continued protection, research, and educational use of the mostly privately owned Santa Cruz Island was granted through a partnership between the Nature Conservancy and the Santa Cruz Island Company.

Giant coreopsis in bloom at Inspiration Point on Anacapa Island, Channel Islands National Park. Photo credit: Robert Schwemmer, NOAA National Marine Sanctuaries.

In 1980, because of its exceptional natural beauty and resources, a portion of the Santa Barbara Channel was given a special protected status with the designation of the Channel Islands National Marine Sanctuary. The sanctuary encompasses Anacapa, Santa Cruz, Santa Rosa, San Miguel and Santa Barbara Islands, extending from mean high tide to six nautical miles (seven miles/11 km) offshore around each of the five islands. The sanctuary's primary goal is the protection of the natural and cultural resources contained within its boundaries. This is an important area for recreational and commercial use, including diving, kayaking, fishing, boating, wildlife viewing, shipping transit, and research.

Container ship EVER GIVEN west bound in the Santa Barbara Channel shipping lanes. Photo credit: Robert Schwemmer, NOAA National Marine Sanctuaries.

Black-and-yellow rockfish in the Channel Islands National Marine Sanctuary.
Photo credit: Claire Fackler, NOAA National Marine Sanctuaries.

Habitat quality and living resource conditions have been degraded somewhat by a variety of human activities, including fishing and boating, as well as changing ocean conditions and disease. The principal threat to maritime archaeological resources in the sanctuary is looting, natural degradation, and the threat of damage from fishing gear or anchors. An additional concern with these historical sites is the fact that, once damaged, there is no potential for recovery, as there is for water, habitat, and living resources.

Céline Cousteau poses with California spiny lobster. Photo credit: Carrie Vonderhaar, Ocean Futures Society.

In 2002 the California Fish and Game Commission established a network of Marine Protected Areas (MPAs) within the nearshore waters of the Channel Islands National Marine Sanctuary. NOAA expanded the MPA network into the sanctuary's deeper waters in 2007. The entire MPA network consists of 11 marine reserves where all take and harvest is prohibited, and two marine conservation areas that allow limited take of lobster and pelagic fish. This MPA network encompasses 318 square miles (823 km²), making it the largest network off the continental United States.

The Channel Islands National Marine Sanctuary is a very unique place at the edge of a human tide. I'm amazed that there are millions and millions of people along the coast and we haven't invaded those islands. It's magic. And now more than before, we're doing the right thing to restore these islands and protect them as a treasure. We've set aside 21 percent of the sanctuary in a network of no-fishing zones and we're finding that it appears to work, although it's very recent. The no-fishing zones act like a nursery where animals grow larger than normal, which means they reproduce more effectively and reproductive capabilities increase exponentially with the size of the fish. The abundance of these zones spills over into adjacent fishing areas, where just outside the boundaries, fishermen can fish all they want. —Jean-Michel Cousteau

More than 20 oil fields and several natural gas fields lie beneath the Santa Barbara Channel in the Santa Barbara Basin. Natural oil seeps in the area are known to have one of the highest rates of seepage in the world. For example, seeps at Coal Oil Point near Santa Barbara are estimated to discharge approximately 150–170 barrels (6,300–7,140 gallons/24,000–27,000 liters) of oil per day. These natural seeps have been chemically analyzed in order to help managers determine whether tar or oil that is found near shore or on beaches comes from a natural seep or from an oil spill. Much of the oil from the seeps accumulates in sediments near the seep itself. Because oil seeps have been occurring for hundreds to thousands of years, plants and animals near the seep have become acclimated to the presence of petroleum compounds.

Oil platform Gail in the Santa Barbara Channel located near the Channel Islands National Marine Sanctuary. Photo credit: Robert Schwemmer, NOAA National Marine Sanctuaries.

Resources within the Channel Islands National Marine Sanctuary

INTERTIDAL ZONE HABITAT

Intertidal zones are composed of a variety of coastal habitats that are periodically covered and uncovered by waves and tides. Therefore, these habitats vary in the type of substrate and degree of exposure to surf. The vertical extent of the tidal change within the Channel Islands can be as much as 10 feet (3 meters). Bottom types in the intertidal zones include fine muds, sand, gravel, cobble, boulders, and bedrock. Sedentary and mobile invertebrates, fish, algae, seabirds, and pinnipeds use the intertidal zone surrounding the Channel Islands. Common invertebrate species include acorn barnacles, periwinkles, limpets, chitons, sea stars, green anemones, shore crabs and California mussels.

Ford Point intertidal zone at Santa Rosa Island, Channel Islands National Marine Sanctuary. Photo credit: Robert Schwemmer, NOAA National Marine Sanctuaries.

HARD AND SOFT BOTTOM SUBTIDAL HABITAT

Subtidal habitats around the islands include those ranging from the lower limit of the intertidal zone down to deepwater offshore. These shallow-water habitats are subject to dynamic physical processes, including wave exposures, along-shore currents, upwelling and suspended sediment loads. Other stresses on intertidal organisms include wide fluctuations in temperature, salinity, and nutrients. Kelp forest rock-bottom and shallow sand-bottom communities make up the predominant nearshore habitats.

Luxuriant forest-like growth of giant kelp occurs in shallow water throughout the sanctuary. The most dense and extensive formations occur along protected island shores and

Male California sheephead in a kelp forest at Gull Island off Santa Cruz Island, Channel Islands National Marine Sanctuary. Photo credit: Robert Schwemmer, NOAA National Marine Sanctuaries.

provide rich habitat for a variety of invertebrate fauna. These species include sponge, kelp crab, spiny lobster, octopus, squid, sea stars and sea urchins. Common fish of the kelp forest include garibaldi, opal eye, kelp bass, California sheephead, sea perch and rockfish.

The two types of marine flowering plants found in the sanctuary form dense beds on different substrate and in different conditions. Surfgrass, found in rocky intertidal and shallow subtidal areas, and eelgrass, found in soft bottom subtidal areas, form productive and complex habitats that provide food and refuge for a wide variety of marine species, including fish and invertebrates that are recreationally and commercially fished. Seagrass beds provide nursery habitat and are important for nutrient cycling and substrate stabilization.

An eelgrass bed off Anacapa Island provides habitat for many species of marine life, Channel Islands National Marine Sanctuary. Photo credit: Robert Schwemmer, NOAA National Marine Sanctuaries.

Rocky subtidal habitats are widespread around the sanctuary, and include high-relief volcanic reefs with walls, ledges, caves, and pinnacles. Low-relief sedimentary reefs exist as well. These rocky subtidal environments are capable of supporting thousands of algal, invertebrate, and fish species, depending on the extent of habitat heterogeneity and influence of physical factors including turbulence, currents, light, temperature, nutrients and sedimentation, and biological interactions such as competition and predation.

Two nudibranchs bristle with protective stinging cells on their backs.
Photo credit: Carrie Vonderhaar, Ocean Futures Society.

Soft bottom habitats are extensive in the sanctuary, especially in deeper water. These habitats support a community living above the sand, including sea pens, sand crabs, sand dollars, sand stars, bottom-dwelling sharks, rays, and flatfishes. In addition, a diverse assemblage also dwells within the soft sediment, including worms, crustaceans, snails, and clams.

DEEP WATER HABITAT

The deep water habitats around the Channel Islands extend from 100 to over 650 feet (30 to more than 200 meters) deep over the continental shelf and slope and well over 3200 feet (1000 meters) in canyons. More than 90 percent of deepwater benthic habitats in the Southern California Bight consist of soft bottom habitat. Most of the deepwater hard bottom substrates are low-relief reefs less than 3 feet (1 meter) in height; some reefs have 3–15 foot (1–5-meter)-high features. Boulders and bedrock outcroppings are features of these reefs in the deep waters around the Channel Islands. Higher relief pinnacles and ridges occur in some areas such as off the northwest end of San Miguel Island. Because of the difficulty in studying very deep habitats, little is known about these areas in the Channel Islands National Marine Sanctuary. However, recent submersible studies have revealed deep sea corals, including a new species, and associated diverse fish and invertebrate communities.

Céline Cousteau investigates a red gorgonian. Though it may look like a brightly colored plant it is actually a colony of filter-feeding animals. Photo credit: Carrie Vonderhaar, Ocean Futures Society.

MARITIME HERITAGE RESOURCES

There are many documented shipwrecks in the waters of the Channel Islands National Marine Sanctuary. One of the oldest documented wrecks is the *Winfield Scott*, a sidewheel passenger steamship that operated during the California Gold Rush. With over 500 passengers heading to Panama from San Francisco, and a load of gold bullion and mail, the ship grounded in dense fog on Anacapa Island in 1853. All passengers were rescued after being stranded on Anacapa Island for about a week. They then boarded the steamer *California* to continue their journey to Panama. This wreck is listed in the National Register of Historic Places. The significant number of shipwrecks within the sanctuary largely can be attributed to prevailing currents and weather conditions, combined with natural hazards.

Paddle wheel flange of Winfield Scott wreck. Photo credit: Robert Schwemmer, NOAA Channel Islands National Marine Sanctuary.

The shipwreck remains reflect the diverse range of activities and nationalities that traversed the Santa Barbara Channel. European sailing and steam vessels, California-built ships of Chinese design called "junks," American coastal traders, vessels engaged in island commerce, and a Gold Rush-era side-wheel steamer have all been lost in sanctuary waters. Each has a story to tell about the history, technology, and society of earlier times.

Between the years 1853 to 1980, an inventory of over 150 historic ship and aircraft wrecks was documented in the Channel Islands National Marine Sanctuary and National Park. To date, about 30 sites have been located and surveyed. The Sanctuary's Shipwreck Reconnaissance Program contributes to scientific knowledge and enhancement of management practices related to underwater archaeological resources by encouraging research and monitoring efforts.

The Ocean Futures Society film team pauses at the stern of the Peacock, sister ship of Captain Jacques-Yves Cousteau's Calypso, in the Channel Islands National Marine Sanctuary. Photo credit: Carrie Vonderhaar, Ocean Futures Society.

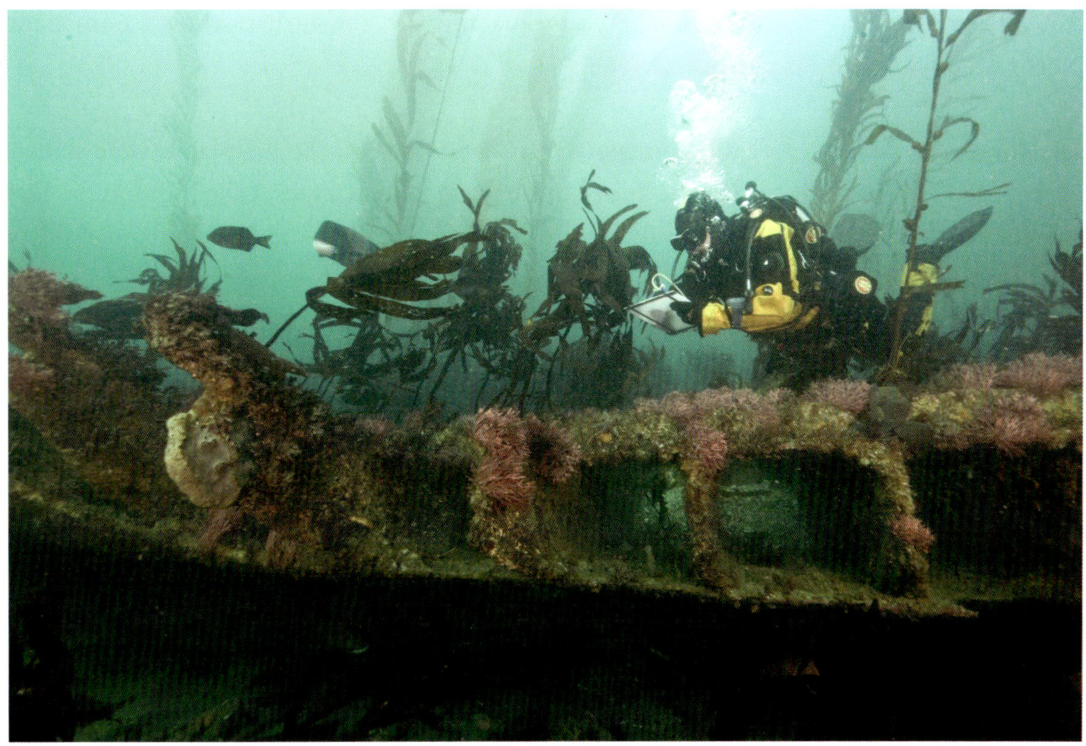

Archaeologist recording the iron hull shipwreck GOLDENHORN lost off Santa Rosa Island in 1892, Channel Islands National Marine Sanctuary. Photo credit: Brett Seymour, National Park Service.

Federally certified scuba divers provide year-round monitoring of submerged sites through cooperative partnerships with the Channel Islands National Park, California State Lands Commission and Coastal Maritime Archaeology Resource organization.

NATIVE PEOPLE

Native peoples have a long history on the Channel Islands. Daisy Cave on San Miguel Island is the site of the oldest known coastal shell midden in North America. This rock shelter was occupied by a series of native peoples over the course of more than 10,000 years. A sample of bone from the remains of "Arlington Springs Man," recovered from

Santa Rosa Island, dates back 13,000 years, making this the earliest-known human in North America.

The Chumash, who lived on the four northern islands and on the mainland, were skilled in making their living from the sea. They built unique plank canoes, called tomols, to fish and collect abalone around the islands, and to trade with peoples on the mainland. And as integral members of an extensive system of trade among various tribes, they collected the shells of *Olivella* snails, which they used as currency. Like other native peoples, the Chumash suffered with the coming of Europeans and others to their lands.

038. Abalone snail. Photo credit: Maia McGuire.

But there are still many people who can trace their ancestry back to these historic Chumash communities. They survived on the strength of their connection with their heritage to the islands, and today they are working to keep that heritage strong and vital. The sanctuary recently partnered with the Chumash community to build the tomol *Elye'wun* (Swordfish) under the leadership of the Chumash Maritime Association. The tomol and its paddlers made an historic journey from the mainland to Santa Cruz Island (known in Chumash as *Limuw*) in 2001—the first such crossing in over 125 years. This crossing has now become an annual event.

Chumash Tomol 'Elye'wun paddlers crossing at Santa Cruz Island. Photo credit: Robert Schwemmer, Channel Islands National Marine Sanctuary.

Key species within the Sanctuary

Squid

To me all of nature is an endless source of inspiration and awe. Our team saw it for themselves in the middle of thousands of mating squid in the Channel Islands, underneath a commercial fishing boat that was hauling squid during their mating and spawning season. Other than the fact that I find squid fascinating, personally I don't like them as a source of food. To me, it's like chewing on my shoe. But they're amazing creatures in the way they change color to communicate and in the massive scale of their reproduction. Squid, cuttlefish and octopus are complicated, intelligent. My father called the octopus the "soft intelligence." The shortfall of these animals is that their lifespan is so short. If they could live as long as we do, as clever as they are, who knows what they could do? Mammals are still the most intelligent, but for coldblooded animals, the squid and octopus are spectacular. An octopus will think a problem through and come up with a solution. Apparently, in the lab they even learn by watching each other from separate tanks. Wow! But I'm very concerned because I think the reason there's an explosion of squid today is because their predators have gone, tuna for instance. As ocean temperatures increase, checks and balances are thrown out of whack. So squid are an indicator of the health of the ocean and even though we enjoy their abundance—and squid are now the biggest fishery in California—from a larger oceanic perspective, it's bad news. That their abundance could be bad news is a paradox, but we have to be careful and watch this fishery.—Jean-Michel Cousteau

While the Ocean Futures Society team prepares for a night dive, a gull takes advantage of the deck lights to catch a meal. Photo credit: Carrie Vonderhaar, Ocean Futures Society.

It had been reported that we had approximately four and possibly six tons of squid underneath the vessel. We knew it was true because we could see them coming to the surface as we shined our lights from the boat. As we dropped in the first five or ten feet (1.5 to 3 meters), there were squid everywhere. You could see them an arm's distance away. By the time we got to about twenty feet (6 meters) we were literally engulfed in a whiteout of squid. They were everywhere. They were in our hands. They were in our faces. They were everywhere, even in our ears. I think they were trying to mate with us! They were rambunctious. They were energetic. They were little creatures of the sea but in a big, giant, squid orgy. You had to literally push squid away from you. It was very disorientating. You had to really pay attention to your gauges because you had no idea of the depth.—Zim Gervais, Marine Operations, Ocean Futures Society.

Ocean Futures Society's marine biologist Holly Lohuis observes market squid in Channel Islands National Marine Sanctuary. Photo credit: Carrie Vonderhaar, Ocean Futures Society.

Squid mate above masses of egg capsules lying on the seafloor. Photo credit: Carrie Vonderhaar, Ocean Futures Society.

The [squid] fishery is now regulated here in California. Scientists believe it's a well-managed, sustainable fishery, and today it's the largest fishery in California. But even so, these squid are vulnerable to natural fluctuations in oceanic conditions. For example, with El Niño events, the squid go to much deeper water and the fishery crashes, but a year later the system changes and colder, nutrient-rich waters return and the squid bounce right back and so does the fishery. —Holly Lohuis, Education/Research Associate, Ocean Futures Society.

Gray whales

The gray whale is probably the best known of the great whales of the northeastern Pacific and the species most frequently seen in and around the Channel Islands National Marine Sanctuary. Adult gray whales reach a length of about 39–46 feet (12–14 meters). Newborn calves tend to be uniformly gray, with the color becoming lighter and more mottled as they mature. Gray whales have no dorsal (back) fin, although they do have six to twelve bumps or ridges along their backs, creating a saw-toothed appearance.

Gray whales are strongly migratory. The majority of southbound gray whales leave the Bering Sea between mid-November and mid-December in groups somewhat segregated by age, sex and class. They swim along the North American Pacific coast during the months of November through January or early February. Some whales do not complete the southbound migrations, instead remaining off the coasts of British Columbia, Washington, Oregon, or California.

Gray whale blowing. Photo credit: Dr. Steven Swartz, NOAA/ NMFS/OPR.

Most of the migrating whales remain close to the coast, in water less than 600 feet (180 meters) deep, until they reach Point Conception, which they typically do between early December and late January. At Point Conception, where the mainland coast makes a sharp eastward turn, about a third of the whales turn to follow the mainland coast, while the remaining two thirds continue directly south, swimming across open waters toward the northern Channel Islands.

Gray whale spyhopping. Photo credit: Matthew Ferraro, Ocean Futures Society.

Most whales pass to the west of San Miguel Island or through the three passes between San Miguel and Santa Rosa Islands, Santa Rosa and Santa Cruz Islands, and Santa Cruz and Anacapa Islands. Vastly more of them swim along the western and southern sides of these islands than along the northern sides.

Whales arrive at Santa Barbara Island from a variety of directions and pass along either (western/eastern) shore. From Santa Barbara Island, most head for Santa Catalina Island and pass along the seaward shore.

Once past the southern Channel Islands (Santa Catalina and San Clemente), most whales return to the coast. Some whales continue on into the Sea of Cortes, but most spend their winters in and near lagoons on the west coast of Baja California and the mainland coast of Mexico near Yavaros.

It has long been believed that most gray whale offspring (calves) are born in Mexican waters in and near the lagoons. But more recent studies have revealed that a higher than expected number of calves are actually born during the southern migration, as far north as southern Oregon. Some mothers and calves have been spotted passing south through the Channel Island sanctuary waters.

Gray whale and calf. Photo credit: Steven Swartz, NOAA/NMFS/OPR.

Gray whales begin leaving the lagoons for the northward migration as early as mid-January; so the beginning of the northbound migration overlaps slightly with the end of the southbound migration near Baja California and Southern California in January and February. The northward migration is shorter than the southward migration, and it occurs in two distinct waves or "pulses." The earlier pulse includes a larger cross section of the whale population. The later, smaller pulse consists primarily of females and their calves.

The occasional observation of females and calves or yearlings in the same kelp areas off the Channel Islands on successive days has led to speculation that quiet kelp beds are of special importance to newborn and juvenile whales during spring. One reason the northbound migration takes longer than the southbound migration is probably due to whales stopping to feed among the kelp beds in the spring.

As with the fall/winter migration, during the spring/summer migration some gray whales do not complete the migration to subarctic or arctic waters, electing instead to spend summer and/or fall in the waters of California, Washington, British Columbia, or Alaska. The number of animals in these "summering" populations appears to be increasing, along with the growth of the population at large (around 19,000 gray whales in the North Pacific as of the most recent population count in 2006/2007).

Footprint and fluke of a gray whale. Photo credit: Carrie Vonderhaar, Ocean Futures Society.

An entangled juvenile gray whale off of Hendrys (Arroyo Burro) Beach, Santa Barbara, CA.
Photo credit: Laura Francis, Channel Islands National Marine Sanctuary.

Xantus's murrelet

The Xantus's murrelet is not only a rarely observed offshore species, it is considered one of the rarest seabirds in the world. These birds are found 65–330 feet (20–100 km) offshore and nest predominantly on rocky ledges, sometimes in dense vegetation. Santa Barbara Island has several nationally and internationally significant seabird nesting areas, including the largest nesting Xantus's murrelet colony. Nesting is concentrated in only four locations, so disruption in these places can be catastrophic for the species. The birds leave their nests only at night to decrease the risk of losing their eggs. Predation by non-native species such as rats (on the Channel Islands) and feral cats (near Baja, California) is a concern to biologists. More than 25% of the world's population of Xantus's murrelets lives in the Santa Barbara region. The primary diet for these birds consists of anchovies, rockfish, crustaceans and fish larvae.

A Xantus's murrelet nesting in rock crevice.
Photo credit: Channel Islands National Marine Sanctuary.

Emerging Environmental Issues

Ship strikes

During the fall of 2007 there were four confirmed blue whale fatalities in the Santa Barbara Channel. Previously, the greatest number of blue whale fatalities in one year off California was three (1988 and 2002 respectively), and these fatalities were separated by hundreds of miles and several months. Of the whales that were examined, including a pregnant adult female with a fetus, all were determined to be struck by ships. The reason for this level of ship strikes in a relatively small area is speculative but may be related to an unusually shallow and/or dense aggregation of krill or increased local density of whales in the Santa Barbara Channel.

Dead blue whale near the Santa Barbara Channel, fall 2007. Photo credit: Todd Jacobs, NOAA.

NOAA Fisheries, the federal agency responsible for protecting marine mammals and endangered marine life, designated the situation as an Unusual Mortality Event (UME). As defined by the Marine Mammal Protection Act, an UME is "a stranding that is unexpected; involves a significant die-off of any marine mammal population; and demands immediate response."

The Sanctuary Advisory Council[1] formed a Ship Strike Subcommittee to develop a Blue Whale/Ship Strike response plan. **NOAA** (including the Channel Island National Marine Sanctuary and National Marine Fisheries Service) and the U.S. Coast Guard are tracking the issue closely and are prepared to respond in the event of a ship strike.

---

1   A sanctuary advisory council is a community-based advisory group consisting of representatives from various user groups, government agencies and the public at large. The role of the council is to provide advice to the sanctuary superintendent on the designation and/or operation of a national marine sanctuary.

Blue whale photographed off the bow of a ship in the Santa Barbara Channel during an aerial survey conducted by staff of the Channel Islands National Marine Sanctuary. Photo credit: Julie Helmers, Office of National Marine Sanctuaries.

Sanctuary staff coordinate, collect and monitor whale sightings in and around the Channel Islands National Marine Sanctuary. Information is obtained from aerial surveys conducted with the U.S. Coast Guard and the California Department of Fish and Game, as well as the Channel Islands Naturalist Corps (CINC) volunteers aboard local whale watch and tour operator vessels. The sightings and general distribution patterns are shared with mariners as well as a variety of agencies and entities, including the National Marine Fisheries Service Office of Protected Resources, US Coast Guard, California Department of Fish and Game, the Santa Barbara Museum of Natural History, the Marine Exchange of Southern California, and whale scientists.

Cargo ships frequently pass by the Channel Islands National Marine Sanctuary. It is strongly recommended that the largest vessels slow to speeds of less than 10 knots as a precaution to avoid striking whales. Photo credit: Carrie Vonderhaar, Ocean Futures Society.

Research Within the Sanctuary

Research projects within the sanctuary include the following:

- Deep-water monitoring of finfish abundance: A remotely-operated vehicle (ROV) is used to take deep-water video of fish within the Channel Islands marine reserves.

- Nesting bird monitoring: **Ashy storm petrels** are thought to number approximately 10,000 worldwide, and over half breed in the Channel Islands. These small seabirds are vulnerable to various human impacts, such as trampling, pollution, lights, and habitat degradation, plus predation by raptors and small mammals. Seabird biologists have been monitoring nests to determine trends in reproductive success and population size. Biologists are also studying nesting Xantus's murrelets on Anacapa Island. These birds nest in caves and crevices, creating challenging conditions for nest monitoring.

- **White Abalone Restoration and Education:** White abalone are large sea snails that are primarily found in deep water off the coast of Southern California. The species has been overfished, and is now experiencing difficulty in reproducing due to the low density and small population. This was the first marine invertebrate to be listed as an endangered species. The restoration plan for this species has four components: locate surviving white abalone by surveying historical habitat; collect brood stock; breed and rear a new generation of juveniles and ultimately, brood stock; and reestablish populations of self-sustaining brood stocks in the wild.

Students on Shearwater with ROV. Photo credit: Claire Fackler, NOAA National Marine Sanctuaries.

Research Assets

The Channel Islands National Marine Sanctuary has a 62-foot (19-meter) high-speed Teknicraft catamaran which is primarily used as a research platform, conducting biotic and abiotic oceanographic research in the waters of the Santa Barbara Channel in Southern California. Its A-frame and winch configuration are used for a variety of projects including trawls, CTD casts, sediment sampling, and towing equipment such as sidescan sonar and ROVs. The wet and dry labs allow on-board processing of samples and data. On board berthing, stowage, galley and safety equipment allow for multiple-day excursions with crews of up to ten scientists.

Readying a CTD (conductivity, temperature and depth) rosette sampler for deployment. Photo credit: Captain Robert A. Pawlowski, NOAA Corps.

Visiting the Sanctuary

Note: In the last section of the book, "When You Visit the Sanctuaries," is detailed information about resources found within each sanctuary to help visitors have an enjoyable and productive visit.

VISITOR'S CENTERS

Outdoors Santa Barbara Visitor Center
113 Harbor Way, 4th Floor
Santa Barbara, CA 93109

The center is staffed by volunteers—please call to find out when the center is open.
Admission is free
Telephone: 805-884-1475

Visitors can enjoy a terrific view from the balcony of this visitor center in Waterfront Center in the Santa Barbara Harbor. Outdoors Santa Barbara Visitor Center is a partnership between Channel Islands National Marine Sanctuary, Channel Islands National Park and the United States Forest Service. Inside the visitor center are interpretive displays about Chumash culture, Spanish explorers, missionaries and American ranchers. A spectacular mosaic tiled floor shows the Channel Islands and the Marine Sanctuary, the Rainbow Bridge legend and flowers native to the islands. An underwater kelp forest mural delights visitors who are curious about the marine life that inhabits the park and marine sanctuary. Garibaldi, tiger sharks, sea stars, lobster, abalone, and urchins are just a few of the species found in the kelp forest mural.

Free brochures and reference materials about the forest, park, sanctuary and the city of Santa Barbara are available for the visitor. A computer screen displays websites of all four agencies for ease in accessing updated information. The outside deck has several interpretive displays about the park, the sanctuary and the forest. A telescope is setup for viewing wildlife and the visitor will find comfortable benches to sit and enjoy the spectacular views from the fourth floor deck. The staff can answer any questions regarding outdoor activities in the area including hiking, camping, diving, kayaking, fishing, surfing, snorkeling, tide pooling, all types of boating, and backpacking.

Santa Barbara Maritime Museum

113 Harbor Way, Suite 190

Santa Barbara, CA 93109

Open every day except Wednesday, from 10am until 6pm.

Closed Christmas Day, New Year's Day, Thanksgiving and the First Friday in August for the Fiesta Parade.

Admission: The third Thursday of every month is free to the public. Free admission is also offered to active duty military members in uniform, infants, and Museum members. Otherwise, a small admission fee is charged.[2]

Telephone: 805-962-8404

The Santa Barbara Maritime Museum features temporary and permanent exhibits designed to highlight the submerged cultural and historic resources located in the Channel Islands National Marine Sanctuary and National Park. Interactive shipwreck exhibits provide the public with the unique opportunity to learn about the region's rich maritime history through historic shipwrecking events and what archaeologists and historians are learning from current field research at the sites. Sanctuary staff participate in ongoing lecture series at the Museum.

Sailing in from the back wall of the Museum is a replica of a Wilson Brothers lumber schooner that contains a state-of-the-art high-definition multimedia theater. The Munger Theater offers a high-tech audio-visual experience for the whole family, with films that take the viewer on underwater adventures, a voyage on a tall ship, deep sea archaeological explorations and much more.

---

2   http://www.sbmm.org/Hours-and-Location/hours-location-and-admission.html

Cabrillo High School Aquarium

4350 Constellation Road

Lompoc, CA 93436

Private tours are available for school groups and other organizations by arrangement. The school offers open house dates (evening hours) several times a year. The dates are listed on the aquarium's website.[3]

Telephone: 805-742-2888

This aquarium is located on the Campus of Cabrillo High School in the Lompoc Unified School District. High school students are active participants in the daily maintenance, operation and outreach programs of the Aquarium. The Sanctuary partners with the Aquarium on exhibits, including a weather kiosk display and other educational programs. Visitors can remotely check out the aquarium through its online "aquarium cam."[4]

Santa Barbara Museum of Natural History's Ty Warner Sea Center

211 Stearns Wharf

Santa Barbara, California, 93101

The Sea Center is open daily between 10:00 AM to 5:00 PM. It is closed on Thanksgiving Day, Christmas Eve (at 3:00 PM), Christmas Day, and New Years Day.

Admission: There is a nominal admission charge.[5]

Telephone: 805-962-2526

The Ty Warner Sea Center (owned and operated by the Santa Barbara Museum of Natural History) is located on Stearns Wharf and fulfills the mission of the Museum to inspire a passion for the natural world. At the Sea Center visitors of all ages can enjoy interactive exhibits, opportunities to work like scientists, a theater showcasing the wonders of the Santa Barbara Channel, hands-on close encounters with sea creatures, and a live shark touch

---

3 http://cabrilloaquarium.org/visitor-info.html
4 http://cabrilloaquarium.org/aquarium-cam.html
5 http://www.sbnature.org/twsc/224.html

pool. Children can crawl through a 1,500-gallon tidepool tank to see ocean life from a different perspective. The Sea Center is an engaging, interactive marine education facility that allows visitors to discover the fun in science and the wonders of the natural world. A webcam allows prospective visitors to check out the aquarium live online.[6]

Exhibits for Channel Islands National Marine Sanctuary at the Ty Warner Sea Center. Photo credit: Laura Francis, Channel Islands National Marine Sanctuary.

---

6   http://www.santabarbara.com/points_of_interest/seacenter/webcam.asp

The Robert J. Lagomarsino Visitor Center at Channel Islands National Park
1901 Spinnaker Drive
Ventura, CA 93001

The fully accessible visitor center is open 8:30 am until 5 pm daily. The visitor center is closed on Thanksgiving and December 25th.
Admission is free.
Telephone: 805-658-5730

The visitor center features a bookstore, a display of marine aquatic life, and exhibits featuring the unique character of each park island. Visitors also will enjoy the 25-minute park movie, "A Treasure in the Sea," shown throughout the day in the auditorium (closed-caption film available upon request).

On weekends and holidays at 11 am and 3 pm, rangers offer a variety of free public programs about the resources of the park.[7]

South Coast Watershed Resource Center
2981 Cliff Drive
Santa Barbara, California 93109

Open every Sunday 10:00 to 4:00 for drop-in visitors. Various water based organizations use the WRC site for meetings, public forums and events. A calendar of events is posted online.[8]
Telephone: 805-884-0459 extension 16

Built at the request of Santa Barbara County in response to growing concern about the South Coast's water quality, the Watershed Resource Center makes the connection between healthy watersheds and individuals' personal habits—such as cleaning up after pets, landscaping with native plants and properly disposing of everyday chemicals. Other fea-

---

7   http://www.nps.gov/chis/planyourvisit/events.htm
8   http://www.artfromscrap.org/pdfs/wrc_events.pdf

tures of the Center include a native plant area, an ocean view deck, a tile mosaic of the Channel Islands, a wetlab for testing water samples, and a special area for the building of a tomol—the traditional redwood plank canoe used by early Chumash people. A research area open to the public includes two on-line computers and a public library. The Watershed Resource Center is housed in a former park ranger station at Arroyo Burro Beach County Park. Throughout the process of redesigning it as a public education facility, the goal was to make it a model of green building principles.

Sanctuary administrative office locations
Santa Barbara Office
Channel Islands National Marine Sanctuary
113 Harbor Way, Suite 150
Santa Barbara, CA 93109
Telephone: 805-966-7107

Southern Office
Channel Islands Harbor
3600 S. Harbor Blvd., Suite 2-202
Oxnard, CA. 93035
Telephone: 805-382-6149

ECO-TOURS

The Channel Islands provides everyone with a plethora of outdoor activities from which to choose. Kayaking to any of the five islands, whether it is for a day trip or for a couple of nights of camping, shows the surrounding marine life in the area and spectacular views of the Santa Ynez Mountains on the mainland. Someone looking for a different view of the islands can join one of the many boat or plane excursions bringing people to the five islands year-round. The islands provide fabulous snorkeling and SCUBA opportunities, especially around Santa Barbara, Anacapa and eastern Santa Cruz Islands, where the diverse kelp forests can be explored in pristine waters. Because of extremely windy conditions, only experienced divers should consider diving off Santa Rosa and San Miguel Islands. Boating, fishing, swimming, and even hiking and whale- and bird-watching can also be explored when visiting the Channel Islands National Marine Sanctuary.

Visitors in the Channel Islands National Marine Sanctuary witnessing birds feeding on anchovies at the surface. Photo credit: Robert Schwemmer, NOAA National Marine Sanctuaries.

Naturalist Corps Instructor. Photo credit: Claire Fackler, NOAA National Marine Sanctuaries.

Channel Islands Naturalist Corps (CINC) is a group of specially trained volunteer ocean stewards dedicated to educating passengers on board vessels visiting the Channel Islands National Marine Sanctuary and Channel Islands National Park. Members provide education about the unique marine life found in sanctuary and park waters to thousands of local residents, tourists, and school children annually. CINC volunteers also participate in numerous local outreach events and collect valuable research on marine mammals and other important sanctuary and park resources. Volunteers accepted into the program are specially trained in a 5-week training class with topics including sanctuary and park resource protection programs, nature interpretation techniques, and an overview of the physical, biological, and cultural aspects of the Santa Barbara Channel and Channel Islands. This program is made possible through a partnership with participating boat operators out of Santa Barbara Harbor, Ventura Harbor, and Channel Islands Harbor.

WHALE WATCHING:

Join Channel Islands Naturalist Corps volunteers on board participating vessels[9] and discover over 28 species of whales and dolphins documented in the sanctuary. See gray whales during their migration between Alaska and Baja from January to April and experience rare and endangered blue whales and humpback whales feeding in the nutrient-rich waters of the sanctuary from May to September.

A whale-watching boat. Photo credit: Josh Kaye-Carr, Channel Islands Naturalist Corps.

---

9   http://channelislands.noaa.gov/edu/edu_vessel.html

VISITING THE CHANNEL ISLANDS

The Channel Islands National Park offers half-day and full-day boat trips to the Channel Islands through their park concessionaires.[10] The islands can be reached by boat or by airplane. There is no transportation available on the islands. Personal watercraft, such as jet skis, are not allowed in park waters.

Arch Point north side of Santa Cruz Island, Channel Islands National Marine Sanctuary. Photo credit: Robert Schwemmer, NOAA National Marine Sanctuaries.

---

10   http://www.nps.gov/chis/planyourvisit/island-transportation.htm

BOATING

Because of challenging weather conditions, boating should not be attempted by the novice or anyone who is not properly trained, conditioned, and equipped. Boaters should always file a formal float plan with the harbormaster before departing. Family and/or friends should also be informed of the float plan. Names and addresses for the boaters, as well as emergency phone numbers, should be listed. Plans should also include the number of boats and boaters on the trip as well as the color, size, and type of craft used. Any survival and special emergency equipment should be listed (EPIRB, VHF, food rations, flares, etc.). The place, date, and time of departure and return should be logged as well as destination(s). This information can be invaluable for a search operation if something goes wrong. Updated navigational charts are available online[11]

Recreational sailboat anchored at Sandstone Point off Santa Cruz Islands, Channel Islands National Marine Sanctuary. Photo credit: Robert Schwemmer, NOAA National Marine Sanctuaries.

---

11   http://www.allisanceforsafenavigation.org/

Sunset over the Channel Islands. Photo credit: Claire Fackler, NOAA National Marine Sanctuaries.

Remember to be flexible with boating plans. Weather should always determine the best course of action. Currents, shifting swells, fog, and strong winds can change quickly in the channel. The trip to the islands also takes boaters across some of the busiest shipping lanes in California. Ship speeds of 25 to 35 knots present a special hazard to boaters crossing the channel. All boaters should listen to the US Coast Guard notice to mariners broadcast on VHF channel 22 because the waters in and surrounding the park are sometimes closed for military operations.

There are no public moorings or all-weather anchorages around the islands. It is recommended that one person stay on board the boat at all times. Boaters are responsible for any damage to the resources caused by their boat. It is recommended that boaters contact the park ranger on each island before landing for an orientation, information on daily events, island safety, landing instructions, weather conditions, or camping check-in. Park rangers occasionally monitor VHF Channel 16. This is a hailing frequency only, and rangers will instruct you to switch to another channel upon contact. If you cannot hail the park ranger on the island on which you plan to land, try contacting one of the other island rangers on a neighboring island, as island canyons and mountains sometimes obscure radio transmission.

Boaters may land according to the following procedures:

<u>Santa Barbara Island</u>: A permit is not required to land or hike on Santa Barbara Island. Access to the island is permitted only at the landing cove. The landing dock is available for unloading purposes only. No craft, including kayaks and inflatables, should be left moored to the dock. Inflatables must be lifted up to the upper landing.

<u>Anacapa Island</u>: A permit is not required to land or hike on East Anacapa Island or at Frenchys Cove. West Anacapa (except Frenchys Cove) is a protected research natural area and is closed to visitors. Visitors are allowed on Middle Anacapa by permit only and when accompanied by a park ranger.

Anacapa Island partially covered by clouds. Photo credit: Robert Schwemmer, NOAA Channel Islands National Marine Sanctuary.

The moorings near the landing cove at East Anacapa Island are reserved for use by the National Park Service (NPS), the US Coast Guard (USCG), and the park concessionaire only. Private boaters must anchor a reasonable distance from these moorings. This is not an all-weather anchorage. It is recommended that one person stay on board the boat at all times. The landing dock is available for unloading purposes only. No craft, including kayaks and inflatables, should be left moored to the dock. Inflatables and kayaks must be lifted up to the lower landing.

<u>Santa Cruz Island</u>: Boaters may land on the eastern 24% of Santa Cruz Island without a permit. This area is owned by the National Park Service and is east of the property line be-

tween Prisoners Harbor and Valley Anchorage. No buoys are available at any landing area. Buoys are reserved for the NPS and the USCG. A pier is available at Scorpion Anchorage and Prisoners Harbor. Due to surf and swell conditions, boaters should use extreme caution when making surf-landings at any beach, especially Smugglers Cove and those beaches facing south and southeast between San Pedro Point and Sandstone Point.

Pelican Bay is a popular recreational boating anchorage at Santa Cruz Island, Channel Islands National Marine Sanctuary. Photo credit: Robert Schwemmer, NOAA National Marine Sanctuaries.

A permit to land on the other 76% of Santa Cruz Island is required from The Nature Conservancy.[12] A fee is charged and no overnight island use is permitted. Allow at least 10 business days for processing.

––––––––––

12   www.nature.org/cruzpermit

<u>Santa Rosa Island</u>: Boaters may land along coastline and on beaches without a permit for day-use only. Beaches between and including Skunk Point and East Point are closed from March 1st to September 15th in order to protect the threatened snowy plover. The beaches around Sandy Point are closed year-round. A pier is available at Bechers Bay. However, boaters may not use the mooring buoys in Bechers Bay. They are reserved for the National Park Service, the Coast Guard, and the park concessionaire.

059. Looking over the Channel Islands from Inspiration Point. Photo credit: Claire Fackler, NOAA National Marine Sanctuaries.

Fast approaching rain squall off Santa Cruz Island, Channel Islands National Marine Sanctuary. Photo credit: Robert Schwemmer, NOAA National Marine Sanctuaries.

<u>San Miguel Island</u>: Overnight anchorages are restricted to Cuyler Harbor and Tyler Bight. Visitors may land only on the beach at Cuyler Harbor. From here, they may walk the beach at Cuyler Harbor and hike up Nidever Canyon to the ranger station. To hike beyond the ranger station, visitors must be escorted by a ranger and have a permit. Visitors should call 805-658-5711 prior to mainland departure to obtain a permit.

Boaters should obtain the latest weather broadcast provided by the NOAA Weather Service by calling (805) 988-6610, visiting Channel Islands National Marine Sanctuary's Internet Weather Kiosk,[13] or by monitoring weather radio on VHF-FM 162.475 MHz (weather

---

13   http://channelislands.noaa.gov/focus/kiosk.html

station 3) for marine forecasts and VHF-FM 162.55 MHz (weather station 1) and VHF-FM 162.40 MHz (weather station 2) for land-based observations. The sanctuary has a boating safety brochure which provides important information for boaters.[14]

Weather conditions vary considerably in the channel. The calmest winds and sea conditions often occur August through October. The other months are subject to a much greater chance for adverse wind and seas with sudden unexpected changes. High winds may occur regardless of the forecast. Forty-knot winds are not unusual for Santa Rosa and San Miguel Islands. Anacapa and Santa Barbara Islands have more moderate winds. Winds are often calm in the early morning and increase during the afternoon. Generally the wind comes from the northwest, but boaters also must be prepared for strong east or Santa Ana winds at anytime, especially from September through April.

Kayakers visiting Little Scorpion Anchorage off Santa Cruz Island, Channel Islands National Marine Sanctuary. Photo credit: Robert Schwemmer, NOAA National Marine Sanctuaries.

14　http://channelislands.noaa.gov/edu/pdf/bas_web1.pdf

Fog bank quickly covering San Miguel Island at Cuyler Harbor, Channel Islands National Marine Sanctuary. Photo credit: Robert Schwemmer, NOAA National Marine Sanctuaries.

Dense fog is common during the summer months, but may occur at any time, making chart and compass navigation mandatory. Ocean currents of considerable strength may be encountered both near and offshore from the islands. Ocean water temperatures range from the lower 50s (°F) in the winter to the upper 60s (°F) in the fall (11–20°C).

Jean-Michel Cousteau at the bow of the Zodiac, Santa Cruz Island, California. Photo credit: Carrie Vonderhaar, Ocean Futures Society.

FISHING

Fishing in the state waters of the Channel Islands (out to 3 nautical miles/3.3 miles/5.5 km) is governed by the State of California. A valid California fishing license with an ocean enhancement stamp is required to fish within this area. There are 11 marine reserves and two conservation areas in the Channel Islands.[15] Fishing is prohibited in the marine reserves, and fishing gear on board a vessel must be stowed and not available for immediate use.

Sport fishing at Talcott Shoal off Santa Rosa Island, Channel Islands National Marine Sanctuary. Photo credit: Robert Schwemmer, NOAA National Marine Sanctuaries.

---

15   http://channelislands.noaa.gov/edu/pdf/pyci-09.pdf

DIVING/SNORKELING

Scuba diving in the kelp forests around the Channel Islands is a unique and different experience for divers more accustomed to tropical waters. Diving in kelp is similar to a walk in a lush forest of trees with these seaweeds growing to heights of more than 120 feet (37 meters). Giant kelp helps support this rare aquatic ecosystem, providing a home for more than 800 species of marine life. The water temperature can vary greatly between the northern and southern ends of the island chain with an average of 50–60°F (10–15.5°C) in winter and 60–70°F (15.5–21°C) in summer. Visibility can range from 40 to 100 feet (12 to 30 meters) and on rare occasions sometimes even up to 150 feet (46 meters).

Diver exploring the lush ecosystem off Anacapa Island, Channel Islands National Marine Sanctuary. Photo credit: Robert Schwemmer, NOAA National Marine Sanctuaries.

065. A young snorkeler weaves her way through giant kelp stalks in the Channel Islands National Marine Sanctuary. Photo credit: Tom Ordway, Ocean Futures Society

Monterey Bay National Marine Sanctuary

About the Monterey Bay National Marine Sanctuary

Monterey Bay National Marine Sanctuary runs along one quarter of the California coastline from Cambria to Marin, encompassing a shoreline length of 276 miles (442 km), and 6,094 square miles (15,783 km^2) of ocean, extending an average distance of 30 miles (48 km) from shore. Designated in 1992, it is the nation's eleventh Marine Sanctuary and its largest—larger then Yosemite or Yellowstone National Parks. As large as the state of Connecticut, at the time of its designation it was the third largest marine protected area in the world.

Sunrise over the hills of Monterey County, from an early departure aboard the R/V Shearwater. Photo credit: Becky Stamski, SIMoN/NOAA.

Its northern shores are lined with pocket beaches and steep bluffs. The shoreline of Monterey Bay itself is a long crescent-shaped beach punctuated in the middle by Elkhorn Slough. Rugged rocky shores line its southern coast where steep mountains rise from the edge of the sea. Underwater, one of its major features is the huge Monterey Canyon. From its head near where Elkhorn Slough meets the bay, the canyon meanders 60 miles (96 km) out to sea, cutting a trench that, at its deepest point, reaches down 12,713 feet (more than two miles or almost 4 km.) In 2009, the sanctuary was expanded to include the Davidson Seamount, an extinct underwater volcano with 200-year-old coldwater corals.

Bubble gum coral at the Davidson Seamount. Photo credit: NOAA/MBARI.

The sanctuary contains a great diversity of habitats and marine life. More than 450 species of algae grow here. Thirty-three species of marine mammals, 94 species of seabirds, 345 species of fish, four species of sea turtles and thousands of invertebrates have been recorded in its waters.

Some live here year round. Others visit seasonally or migrate through. When the California Current runs strongly, it carries cold-water animals down from the north. When it weakens in late summer, the warm water brings sea turtles, swarms of jellies and other plants and animals up from the south.

Heermann's gulls. Photo credit: Chad King, Monterey Bay National Marine Sanctuary.

Without even stepping foot on a boat you can witness its incredible marine life from shore— whales, sea otters, harbor seals, sea lions, pelicans, and a variety of marine life abound. Some 2,000 sea otters live in kelp beds along the coast here. In winter and spring, gray whales can be spotted from high bluffs. Visitors who venture offshore in boats can find blue and humpback whales, along with seabirds, killer whales and other dolphins. Divers find kelp forests filled with fishes and invertebrates. The sanctuary's rich waters also support important commercial and sport fisheries for market squid, salmon, rockfish and other species.

Just a short walk from the parking lot down the Breakwater in Monterey, dozens of California sea lions sunbathe on the rocks. Photo credit: Carrie Vonderhaar, Ocean Futures Society.

The Monterey Bay National Marine Sanctuary contains about 225 documented shipwrecks[1] or lost aircraft, and is thought to have more than 1000 undocumented shipwrecks. There are 718 historic sites within the sanctuary.

---

1   http://channelislands.noaa.gov/shipwreck/dbase.html

Why a National Marine Sanctuary?

The marine environment off the central California coast was designated as a national marine sanctuary because its unique biological, geological, and oceanographic features make it one of the richest marine environments in the world. Monterey Bay National Marine Sanctuary was established for the purpose of resource protection, research, education and public use. Its natural resources include a large kelp forest, one of North America's largest underwater canyons and the closest-to-shore deep ocean environment in the continental United States. It is home to one of the most diverse marine ecosystems in the world. This remarkably productive marine environment is fringed by spectacular coastal scenery, including sandy beaches, rocky cliffs, rolling hills and steep mountains.

Little Sur Beach. Photo credit: Steve Lonhart, NOAA Monterey Bay National Marine Sanctuary.

Activities that put pressure on sanctuary resources are diverse. Some of the most prominent pressures include vessel traffic, commercial and recreational fishing, agricultural and urban runoff, harmful algal blooms, coastal development, marine debris, the introduction of non-indigenous species, and disturbances to wildlife.

Water quality parameters in the offshore environment of the sanctuary suggest degraded conditions. The main contributors to degraded water quality conditions are land-based activities, such as those linked to urban development and agriculture that input contaminants and nutrients into offshore sanctuary waters, and vessel traffic that can result in the discharge of ballast water, bilge oil, and marine debris.

One of Celebrity's cruise ships, the Infinity, anchored inside of Monterey Bay. This anchoring site is one of two designated by MBNMS that avoid sensitive habitat. Passengers are ferried to the streets of Monterey via a boat tender, pictured here on the right. Photo credit: Chad King / Monterey Bay National Marine Sanctuary.

Habitat modification has occurred in the offshore environment of the sanctuary; the most significant physical alteration of sanctuary habitats has likely resulted from fishing with bottom-contact gear, such as otter trawls. Among the various environmental impacts resulting from use of this type of gear are removal of structure-forming organisms and the smoothing of bedforms. A variety of recent management measures directed towards trawling may allow for an improvement in the condition of offshore habitats due to some recovery of seafloor habitats in the areas that were previously trawled.

The health of several key species has been compromised by exposure to neurotoxins produced by harmful algal blooms, entanglement in active and lost fishing gear, ingestion of marine debris, and accumulation of persistent contaminants. Recent management actions to reduce marine debris and to recover overfished stocks and impacted habitats were implemented to improve the state of living resources, and in some cases they have begun to do so.

Lost fishing gear laid out on the US Coast Guard pier. Photo credit: Karen Grimmer, Monterey Bay National Marine Sanctuary.

There is great uncertainty regarding the integrity of submerged maritime archaeological resources in the offshore environment in the sanctuary. The sanctuary's inventory contains information on known vessel losses, with little to no verified location information, and few visited sites. In addition, the National Oceanic and Atmospheric Administration has conducted only one offshore archaeological site location inventory in the sanctuary.

The Mission Statement: "The mission of the Monterey Bay National Marine Sanctuary (MBNMS) is to understand and protect the coastal ecosystem and submerged cultural resources of central California."

Resources within the Monterey Bay National Marine Sanctuary

ROCKY SHORELINES

The Monterey Bay National Marine Sanctuary's rocky shores are characterized by a fascinating and diverse array of intertidal organisms. The dramatic influence of the tidal cycle exposes intertidal invertebrates and algae to large fluctuations in temperature, desiccation and wave action twice per day. This range of environmental variables in turn interacts with biological factors to create the distinct zonation patterns evident on any trip to the rocky shore.

The rocky coast of the Monterey Bay National Marine Sanctuary provides the perfect opportunity for tidepool exploration. Photo credit: Carrie Vonderhaar, Ocean Futures Society.

Individual species tend to occupy different parts of the intertidal gradient from the high intertidal zone, where environmental stress is highest, to the low intertidal zone, where biological interactions prevail. The striking vertical range occupied by these organisms has long motivated scientists and visitors to investigate the abundant and species-rich assemblage of intertidal organisms that thrive in the sanctuary. Many of the 150[+] marine species found on the rocky shore do not occur subtidally, contributing to the unique nature of this habitat at the interface of land and ocean.

Rocky shores make up 33 percent of sanctuary shoreline habitat and primarily occur near the tips of and outside Monterey Bay, extending southward along the Big Sur coast and north toward San Francisco.

A crab blows bubbles to keep its gills moist in the intertidal zone. Photo credit: Maia McGuire.

BEACHES

Beaches are one of the most visible and popular sanctuary habitats. They offer opportunities for beach volleyball, surfing, picnicking, fishing and windsurfing. Sand beaches represent half the intertidal habitat in the Monterey Bay National Marine Sanctuary. Every year, travelers from around the world come to enjoy the natural scenery, wildlife and recreation that the sanctuary's beaches offer. Unfortunately, beaches suffer from a number of challenges. These include water quality, coastal armoring and trash.

McWay Cove in Julia Pfeiffer Burns State Park. Looking from the trail that parallels the cove. McWay waterfall. Photo credit: Steve Lonhart, NOAA Monterey Bay National Marine Sanctuary.

KELP FORESTS

Kelp forests extend throughout most of the nearshore waters of the Monterey Bay National Marine Sanctuary. Hugging the coastline, they extend from just beyond the breaking waves to depths of about 100 feet (30.5 meters). Although kelp forests are a familiar and iconic habitat within the sanctuary, kelp canopy cover typically encompasses about 25 square miles (65 km²), or less than 0.5% of the total surface area within the sanctuary.

Monterey Bay National Marine Sanctuary Kelp Beds: Square Black Rock. Photo credit: Steve Lonhart, NOAA Monterey Bay National Marine Sanctuary.

CONTINENTAL SHELF

In the Monterey Bay National Marine Sanctuary, the outer continental shelf is relatively broad from the northern boundary to southern Monterey Bay. The shelf narrows considerably south of Monterey Bay and remains narrow throughout most of the southern portion of the sanctuary, except around Point Sur and near the southern boundary.

A large portion of the shelf in the sanctuary is composed of soft-bottom habitats. Soft-bottom associated species live either on the surface of, or buried in, the sediments. Some of these animals, such as the burrowing tube anemone, build somewhat permanent tubes and burrows. The burrowing activities of fishes and invertebrates help to mix the surface sediments and also add some structural relief to a relatively flat habitat. Occasional rock outcrops, in an otherwise soft-bottom habitat, provide substrate for large sessile, sedentary and habitat-forming invertebrates, including white-plumed anemones, crinoids and basket stars.

Several white-plumed anemones growing adjacent to club-tipped anemones.
Photo credit: Chad King, SIMoN/NOAA.

Gopher rockfish. Photo credit: Steve Lockhart, NOAA Monterey Bay National Marine Sanctuary.

The rocky habitat that speckles the seafloor between the edge of the kelp forest and the continental shelf break (100 to 656 feet/30 to 200 meters) covers approximately 96 square miles (249 square kilometers)—only 1.8 percent of the seafloor in the sanctuary. Rock outcrops below 100 feet (30 meters) are teeming with life. Small forms of brown and red algae grow on rock outcrops down to a depth of between 200 and 250 feet (60 and 75 meters) off Point Sur, depending on the clarity of the water. Sessile invertebrates cover the rocky bottom, supplying food and shelter to many mobile invertebrate and fish species.

The complex physical structure created by boulders, caves, pinnacles and outcrops is a favorite habitat of many rockfish species. Pelagic predators, including seabirds and marine mammals, hunt for fishes and invertebrate prey along the benthos.

ESTUARIES

Estuaries represent the confluence of terrestrial, freshwater and marine ecosystems, creating multiple unique habitats that support highly diverse communities and provide important ecosystem services. Unfortunately, these rare but highly productive areas are also very fragile, and human encroachment has compromised their ability to provide biological services (e.g., nursery and feeding grounds for fishes and birds) and has diminished their ability to act as an environmental filter.

Kayakers in the Slough. Photo credit: Steve Lonhart, NOAA Monterey Bay National Marine Sanctuary.

Within or immediately adjacent to the Monterey Bay National Marine Sanctuary there are 26 estuarine habitats identified by the U.S. Fish and Wildlife Service and listed in its National Wetlands Inventory. The largest estuary in the sanctuary is Elkhorn Slough, which serves as an important resting and/or feeding stop for migratory bird species using the Pacific Flyway. Elkhorn Slough also serves an important role in sustaining resident birds that use the resources generated by this highly productive ecosystem.

Designated in 2000 as a Globally Important Bird Area by the American Bird Conservancy, Elkhorn Slough is world-renowned among avid bird watchers for its diversity and abundance of birds. After San Francisco Bay, Elkhorn Slough has one of the largest remaining salt marshes in California. Its estuarine habitats host more than 100 fish and more than 400 invertebrate species as well as marine mammals, including dozens of southern sea otters.

A long-billed curlew searches for a meal in the shallow water.
Photo credit: Carrie Vonderhaar, Ocean Futures Society.

SEAMOUNTS

Seamounts are mainly volcanic in origin, rising to considerable height from great depths along the continental rise and are limited in length across the summit.

Seamounts, though common in the world's oceans, often have very different biological assemblages than the surrounding seafloor sediments, due likely to the complex, rocky and current-swept habitats. Rocky outcrops, particularly near seamount peaks, are inhabited by a suite of deep-sea corals and sponges that are usually absent or quite rare in more typical ocean settings.

Crinoids, black corals, primnoid corals, mushroom soft corals, sea stars, bryozoans, and anemone on the Davidson Seamount at 8753 feet (2668 meters) depth. Photo credit: NOAA/MBARI 2006.

In March of 2009, NOAA designated the Davidson Seamount Management Zone, increasing the Monterey Bay National Marine Sanctuary and protecting Davidson Seamount, making it the first seamount within a national marine sanctuary. Assemblages of large corals and sponges, along with many associated animals such as sea stars, anemones, crustaceans, octopus and fishes, are common on the seamount. Recent explorations have discovered several species new to science. Ecological processes influencing the distribution, abundance and dynamics of seamount fauna are less well known than other charismatic ecosystems, such as kelp beds and corals reefs, making it difficult to develop management criteria.

SUBMARINE CANYONS

Submarine canyons are the most prominent geomorphic features within the Monterey Bay National Marine Sanctuary.

Monterey Canyon, in the center of Monterey Bay, is the largest submarine canyon along the coast of North America. Similar in size to the Grand Canyon in Arizona, it is 4,292 miles (70 kilometers) long and approximately 7.5 miles (12 kilometers) at its widest point, with a maximum rim to floor relief of 5,577 feet (1,700 meters). Numerous smaller canyons cut into the continental shelf and slope of the sanctuary. The walls and floors of submarine canyons cover approximately 840 square miles (2,175 square kilometers), or 16 percent, of the sanctuary seafloor. The great majority of canyon habitat is soft-bottom; a much smaller portion is hard-bottom.

Most organisms observed in canyons are not unique to canyon systems but are also found at similar depths outsides canyons. However, because submarine canyons extend from shallow waters of the continental shelf to the deep sea and contain a wide range of habitats, they contain an incredible diversity of organisms.

Young of the year spotted ratfish observed in Carmel canyon during a sanctuary seafloor monitoring survey using the Delta *submersible.* **Photo credit:** *Jean DeMarignac, SIMoN/NOAA.*

Mobile fishes and invertebrates, such as prickly sharks and krill, have been found to aggregate in canyon heads and along canyon walls. Rocky outcrops along canyon walls are colonized by invertebrates—including feather stars, corals and tunicates—and provide shelter for a variety of rockfishes. Clams and worms burrow into canyon walls. The soft sediments on the canyon floor support a diverse community of invertebrates (e.g., sea pens, sea cucumbers, brittle stars, sea stars) and fishes (e.g., flatfishes, ratfishes, whiptails, grenadiers, sablefish, hake, and thornyheads).

An unidentified yellow sponge near Grimes Canyon along the Big Sur coast. **Photo credit:** *Chad King, SIMoN/ NOAA.*

DEEP SEA HABITAT

The deep sea is a dark, cold environment that includes a variety of habitats from the mid-water region to the abyss; these are populated by a wide array of animals that are specially adapted to live under the tremendous water pressure and low oxygen level of this harsh environment. In recent years, improved sampling techniques and technologies have shown that the diversity of deep-sea fauna is greater than once thought.

Bathysaur. Photo credit: NOAA/MBARI.

The deep sea begins at the continental shelf break, at a depth of approximately 650 feet (200 meters). Beyond the shelf break, the continental slope descends through the deep sea to the ocean floor. Of the total seafloor area in the sanctuary, approximately two-thirds (3,538 square miles, or 9,164 square kilometers) are located in the deep sea. This region also encompasses two distinct pelagic zones: the mesopelagic zone, which starts 656 feet (200 meters) below the surface and extends to about 3,280 feet (1,000 meters); and the bathypelagic zone, from 3,280 feet (1,000 meters) down to the seafloor.

Although the deep sea encompasses 98 percent of all living space on the planet by volume, it is among the least understood ecosystems because of the challenges inherent in accessing it. Marine scientists claim that we know more about space than we do about this remote environment. To reach the ocean's depths, scientists require a platform from which to deploy sampling or observational gear. Today, in addition to net sampling, manned and unmanned research submersibles are deployed from research ships to collect data and make observations in this remote environment.

The deep sea comes very close to shore in the sanctuary through the heads of several canyons (Monterey Canyon is the largest), making deep water relatively easy to access here.

Submersible Delta on the deck of the R/V Velero. Photo credit: Chad King, Monterey Bay National Marine Sanctuary.

NATIVE PEOPLE

Like other native people along the Pacific Coast, the Ohlone of California's central coast drew their living from both land and water for 10,000 years or more. The Monterey Bay area provided acorns for food, and willows and other plants for basket making. The sea supplied fish, birds, sea lions and other marine mammals and many kinds of shellfish. Despite the devastation of their culture and the loss of their lands, there are still some 500 Ohlone today, most living in their ancestral area. Though few in number, they continue to thrive as a tribe and still carry on native traditions.

Two male elephant seals fight for dominance. Photo credit: Carrie Vonderhaar, Ocean Futures Society.

Key Species within the Sanctuary

ELEPHANT SEALS

Winter is the only window of opportunity that elephant seals have to mate. Once they leave Piedras Blancas,[2] male and female elephant seals will embark on separate long-distance migrations of over 10,000 miles (16,000 km) to destinations far in the middle of the Pacific Ocean and north to the Aleutian Islands. They will spend 80 to 90 percent of their lives in the open sea foraging for food: skates, sharks, hake, crab, and squid, and diving to extraordinary depths of 5,000 feet (1524 meters) or more to reach their prey. But their gracefulness in the sea is lost on land. Gravity and their gigantic mass make their lumbering forms on the beach appear clumsy by comparison. Bulls are typically twice the size of females, and their size and weight would pose risks to the colony's nursing mothers and vulnerable pups if blind mating urges were to go unchecked.

But in infinite variations of balance and counter balance, nature has evolved a strategy for dealing with these unruly bulls. By clustering together, elephant seal mothers gain protection from predators and the harassment of bachelor males and, by defending these harems, only the fittest bulls earn mating access.

As the males arrive on the beach each November, the colony's ground rules are quickly re-established. Dominance displays lead to battles, with only the winners earning harems. Losers are forced into retreat and may form lonely looking groups on separate bachelor beaches. Female elephant seals ready to give birth arrive a month later, and the first pups are usually born by Christmas. The young seals are weaned after only 28 days, but will remain on the beach for another two to three months after the mothers, who've been fasting since their arrival, depart for the sea. Dominant alpha males, called beach masters, will mate with the females of their harem as they attempt to leave the nurseries. Young bachelors that lurk too long or dare to trespass receive

---

2   Piedras Blancas, seven miles north of San Simeon on the California coast, is a rookery that is home to about 15,000 elephant seals in the winter months.

bellowed warnings from the beach master's magnificently inflated proboscis, an instrument of vocal combat that, if unheeded, can lead to a violent charge. These winter days devoted to birth and mating are the only moments northern elephant seals will spend on land for the entire year. During the 1800s though, it was sufficient time for the predator that hunted them to the edge of extinction.

Male elephant seal mating with a female. Photo credit: Denise Kocek.

Scientists can't say for certain what the population of northern elephant seals was before the turn of the twentieth century. In their home range from Baja California, Mexico, to Alaska, they had few natural predators, only transient orcas and migrating white sharks. Until the arrival of Europeans, they were hunted only on subsistence scales by coastal tribes for hides, food and blubber. But by the time of California's

Gold Rush in 1849, exploration of the western United States had ceded to full-scale exploitation. Sperm whales had been targeted so relentlessly, and gray whales, the "devil fish," were so dangerous that the whaling business was in decline. But the need for oil and lubricants fueled by the Gold Rush was still expanding.

Whalers turned their attention toward the shore and found that the blubber of elephant seals rendered high-quality oil and…an easy kill. It took only 15 breeding seasons to finish them off.

By the late 1870s, elephant seals were believed to be extinct. But a scientific expedition to Isla Guadalupe, off the coast of Baja California, uncovered nine elephant seal survivors. Seven were promptly killed, however, for museums back home. Yet, somehow, the species persisted, perhaps because of the protection the open sea afforded them during their migrations. Years later, in 1911, a breeding colony of several hundred elephant seals were again found on the same island. This led Mexico to establish the Isla Guadalupe Biosphere Reserve in 1922.

With its first breath the pup vocalizes securing a bond with its mother. It is this vocalization that allows mother and pup to find each other amongst the hundreds of other Northern elephant seals crowding the beach. Photo credit: Carrie Vonderhaar, Ocean Futures Society.

There is no waste in nature. A gull feeds on a newborn pup's umbilical cord. Photo credit: Carrie Vonderhaar, Ocean Futures Society

This tiny preserve and progressive conservation measures are credited with saving the entire species. Today's survivors are all descendents of the Guadalupe colony. In less than 100 years, northern elephant seals have rebounded to approximately 175,000 animals and recovered nearly all of their former range. The colony at the San Simeon rookery at the southern end of Monterey Bay National Marine Sanctuary, has grown from a few animals to over 13,000 in just 15 years.

But there are concerns that elephant seals might not be in the clear yet. Questions still linger over what the consequences of being forced through a genetic bottleneck might pose for populations. For scientists that means a wait-and-see approach with fingers crossed that the loss of genes and inbreeding don't hold hidden pitfalls for elephant seals' long-term recovery.

An elephant seal mother fasts for the 4 weeks she nurses her pup. Once the pup is weaned she returns to the sea and leaves the pup to fend for itself. Photo credit: Carrie Vonderhaar, Ocean Futures Society.

Ocean warming may also pose problems for elephant seals.... Changes in sea temperatures can widely affect the distribution and availability of food. And, when female seals have "to spend more time looking for prey and are less successful in acquiring it," they have less fat reserves to produce the rich milk their pups depend on for survival.

Working with northern elephant seals, conservationists are learning that protection from exploitation and preserving critical habitat are the best chances for a species on the brink.

Report abandoned sea otter pups to the Monterey Bay Aquarium's Sea Otter Rescue and Care Program at 831-648-4829. These groups will be able to determine the best course of action for the animals.

A seal or sea lion pup found alone on the beach is generally not an abandoned animal. People who come across a pup on the beach should leave it. Any attempt to move it may cause the person or the pup to get hurt, or cause the mother to abandon the pup. Report injured or distressed sea lion pups to the Marine Mammal Center Hotline at 831-633-6298 or 415-289-7350.

Weaners are pups no longer nursing on their mother's milk and at the end of the season are the only ones left on the beach. Photo credit: Matthew Ferraro, Ocean Futures Society.

SAND CRABS

Sandy beach monitoring in the West Coast marine sanctuaries focuses on the sand crab, or Pacific mole crab—a common inhabitant. Sand crabs, which filter-feed plankton from the water, are important organisms in this ecosystem. They are eaten by coastal birds and sea otters. Sand crabs are used by humans as bait for fishing and have been used as indicators of the pesticide DDT and the neurotoxin domoic acid. The sand crab is also an intermediate host for a number of parasites, including acanthocephalans (thorny-headed worms), which affect threatened sea otters and surf scoters (sea ducks).

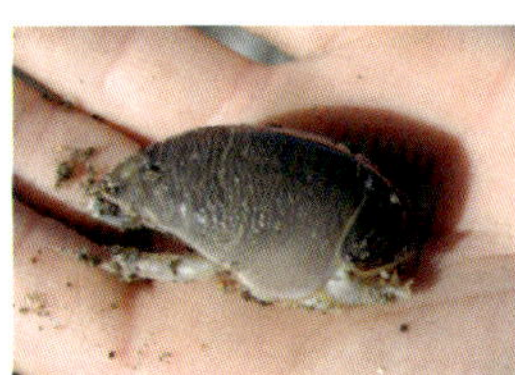

Sand crabs extend their elegant, feathery antenna to filter nutrients from sea water in the wave wash zone. Photo credit: Amy Dean.

A southern sea otter rests in the reflection of a sailboat at Elkhorn Slough.
Photo credit: Carrie Vonderhaar, Ocean Futures Society.

Emerging Environmental Issues

MICROCYSTIN TOXIN

Scientists from the California Department of Fish and Game and the University of California Santa Cruz have discovered that a toxin produced by freshwater bacteria is entering the ocean and poisoning sea otters. This study is significant because it is the first to establish a connection between freshwater contamination by the toxin microcystin and marine mammal mortality. Researchers report that the deaths of at least 21 southern sea otters (a federally listed threatened species found only in California) were linked to microcystin. The toxin is produced by a bacterium called *Microcystis,* also known as blue-green algae, which thrives in warm, stagnant, nutrient-rich water.

Students monitoring water quality. Photo credit: Claire Fackler, NOAA National Marine Sanctuaries.

The team found high concentrations of microcystin in lakes bordering Monterey Bay and in rivers that flow into the bay. The toxin was also detected in ocean water at the Santa Cruz wharf.

Many of the microcystin-poisoned sea otters were recovered near river mouths and harbors. While most of the cases (17) occurred within Monterey Bay, microcystin-poisoned sea otters were also found along the Big Sur and south-central California coastlines. Microcystin poisoning can cause acute liver failure or damage other tissues and can be fatal.

Laboratory studies show that filter-feeding shellfish, such as mussels and clams, that are exposed to water containing microcystin will accumulate the toxin in their tissues. The toxin remains in the tissues for up to two weeks, even if the source is removed. It is felt that otters become exposed to the toxin by feeding on contaminated shellfish. Humans also may be at risk from microcystin poisoning if they consume shellfish harvested near river mouths, especially during or after periods of freshwater runoff. Further studies are needed to more accurately assess the potential for risks to human health.

Jean DeMarignac (SIMoN Scientist) and Erica Burton (MBNMS Research Analyst) planning the next dive of the submersible "Delta" aboard the R/V Velero. Photo credit: Chad King, Monterey Bay National Marine Sanctuary.

The toxin should not be a concern for commercially-harvested shellfish which come from areas unlikely to be contaminated by the toxin. Drinking water systems seek to avoid algal growth in their sources because of foul taste and odor. To date, there have been no known human illnesses linked to microcystin exposure in shellfish or drinking water.

Research Within the Sanctuary

Research in the Monterey Bay National Marine Sanctuary is focused on protecting the habitats and species within the sanctuary. Current research projects include the following:

- Pathogen and contaminants research: Research is underway to develop new, more rapid methods for detecting waterborne pathogens to allow managers to adequately protect beach visitors

- Bottom trawling—habitat and species recovery: Trawling activities are no longer permitted within the sanctuary; this research is studying the recovery of habitats that were damaged by trawling activities, as well as the recovery of species within those habitats.

- Harmful algal blooms: Harmful algal blooms (HABs) are a naturally occurring event on the West Coast. In the last 30 years they have increased in both frequency and intensity. Impacts include threats to marine wildlife, economic losses to fisheries and tourist industries, and human health. By studying the population structure of these potentially toxic species, researchers hope to gain a better understanding of the mechanisms that control the distribution and toxicity of HABs.

- Habitat characterization: Researchers are studying the habitat and organisms associated with the Davidson Seamount and the continental shelf in order to assess management needs for resource protection.

- Sanctuary Integrated Monitoring Network (SiMON): Monterey Bay National Marine Sanctuary is part of the SiMON network.[3]

---

3   http://www.sanctuarysimon.org/

Visiting the Sanctuary

Note: In the last section of the book, "When You Visit the Sanctuaries," is detailed information about resources found within each sanctuary to help visitors have an enjoyable and productive visit.

Monterey Bay National Marine Sanctuary is home to miles of undeveloped beaches, an underwater canyon, the nation's largest kelp forest, and many more natural habitats that are just waiting to be explored. Visitors can take a boat trip to watch the varied marine wildlife, including whales, sea otters, seals, sea lions, and birds. The water's secrets can also be discovered by sea kayaking, diving, snorkeling, sailing or boating. Closer to the shore, visitors can surf, fish or go tidepooling. Other options include bird-watching at Elkhorn Slough, the second-largest coastal wetland in California, visiting numerous state beaches and coastal state reserves with miles of undeveloped beaches, hiking trails, and two visitor-accessible breeding colonies of Northern elephant seals, or learning about the local marine ecosystem at the Monterey Bay Aquarium in Monterey or the Seymour Marine Discovery Center in Santa Cruz. From surfing to diving and hiking to boating, Monterey Bay provides recreation that can grab anyone's attention.

A father and son gaze upon the large swells hitting the Monterey Peninsula. Photo credit: Chad King, Monterey Bay National Marine Sanctuary.

VISITOR'S CENTERS
Coastal Discovery Center[4] at San Simeon Bay
Building 1 Hearst State Beach at San Luis Obispo San Simeon Road
San Simeon, CA 93452

Mailing address: P.O. Box 116
San Simeon, CA 93452

The Coastal Discovery Center is open to the public free of charge every Friday, Saturday and Sunday during the summer from 11 a.m. to 5 p.m., and Saturday and Sundays during the winter months from 10 a.m. to 4 p.m. It is also open during most holiday Mondays. School group programs are offered during the week and arranged by appointment.
Admission is free
Telephone: 805-927-6575

Mural on the side of the Coastal Discovery Center. Photo credit: Carolyn Skinder, Monterey Bay National Marine Sanctuary.

The Coastal Discovery Center at San Simeon Bay is an environmental and nature center cooperatively operated by the Monterey Bay National Marine Sanctuary and California State Parks. It is located at historic William R. Hearst Memorial Beach in San Simeon, a popular site for picnicking, swimming, hiking, fishing from the pier and viewing marine wildlife. The Center is in close proximity to the Hearst Castle, California's largest elephant seal rookery, and the Piedras Blancas Light Station.

---

4   www.coastaldiscoverycenter.org

The Coastal Discovery Center offers information on natural and cultural resources along the central California coast. The Center's primary function is to provide education and outreach to the general public and to school groups about the natural and cultural resources of coastal California.

Exhibits include natural and cultural resources, watersheds, deep sea voyages, elephant seals, and a tidepool.

Recurring public programs include presentations about the **history of San Simeon Bay** on San Simeon Pier the first weekend of each month from 11 a.m. to 1 p.m., and the **Coastal Discovery Fair on the** third Saturday in July each year.

The interactive talking tidepool exhibit represents the animals along the rocky shore, the interface between the land and the sea. Photo credit: Monterey Bay National Marine Sanctuary.

Sanctuary Exploration Center (Santa Cruz)

A 12,000-square-foot Sanctuary Exploration Center is under construction in Santa Cruz' famed beach area. The Exploration Center is expected to open in 2012. The facility is being constructed following the certification standards of Leadership in Energy and Environmental Design (LEED). Plans for the center call for exhibits, classroom, administrative space and a gift shop.

Exploration Center Goals:
- Involve and educate visitors about the sanctuary's unique and fascinating coastal and marine natural resources
- Instill in visitors a sense of personal stewardship with regard to the sanctuary and an understanding of how to help protect it
- Provide orientation for visitors as they enter the sanctuary, so they will use and enjoy it in a responsible and sensitive manner
- Construct an environmentally sensitive building that will demonstrate the advantages of sustainability

Artist's rendering of the new Sanctuary Exploration Center. Credit: Monterey Bay National Marine Sanctuary.

Led up the stairs by the sound of wind, waves and gulls, visitors climb a stairway lined with beautiful images of the Monterey Bay National Marine Sanctuary (MBNMS). A window on the Landing allows visitors to see into a water-filled tank re-creating a part of the Monterey Submarine Canyon. They can also reach this mid-level by taking the elevator from the first floor.

At the top of the stairs, visitors may go onto the deck or interact with an enticing video kiosk that describes the 14-site National Marine Sanctuary program. Nearby, graphic panels introduce the Monterey Bay National Marine Sanctuary, including a site relief map, a brief explanation of what they will see in the galleries and highlights of some of the activities going on at the sanctuary.

Inside the Exploration Center, interactive exhibits profile sanctuary research, including deep sea exploration, habitats and wildlife in the Monterey Bay National Marine Sanctuary, and connections between human activities and environmental health of the sanctuary.

Coastal Interpretive Signage (Monterey Bay Sanctuary Scenic Trail)
Sanctuary interpretive signage is installed in numerous locations along the coast in partnership with California State Parks, U.S. Forest Service, Cities of Monterey and Pacific Grove, Cambria Community Services District, Bureau of Land Management and many more. The scenic trail enables visitors to explore and enjoy the coastline from Santa Cruz to Monterey, and enhance appreciation and protection of the sanctuary through engaging interpretative information.

Volunteers wearing bright blue BayNet jackets can be found at Lighthouse Point on West Cliff Drive. They will share their binoculars and answer questions about local wildlife and the ecology of the Monterey Bay National Marine Sanctuary.

Sanctuary administrative office locations
Monterey Office:
299 Foam Street
Monterey, CA 93940
Telephone: 831-647-4201

San Simeon Office:
Hearst Memorial State Beach
P.O. Box 116
San Simeon, CA 93452
Telephone: 805-927-2145

Santa Cruz Office:
110 Shaffer Road
Santa Cruz, CA 95060
Telephone: 831-420-3663

WHALE WATCHING

Thanks to its nutrient-rich waters, the Monterey Bay National Marine Sanctuary offers some of the world's best whale watching.

During the winter and spring months, the entire gray whale population migrates through the sanctuary within two miles (three kilometers) of the Monterey Bay coastline, traveling to their summer feeding grounds in the Bering Sea and to their winter breeding grounds in Baja. Gray whales are rarely seen feeding in central California. Gray whales, especially calves, fall prey to killer whales and these events sometimes occur within the sanctuary.

A pod of transient orca attempts to separate a gray whale mother and calf.
Photo credit: Matthew Ferraro, Ocean Futures Society.

During the summer and fall months, blue whales and humpback whales migrate to the sanctuary to feed on their primary prey of anchovies and krill. Blue whales have been observed feeding on dense swarms of krill near Monterey and the Farallones. Humpback whales are one of the most common large baleen whales seen in the sanctuary, but California estimates are significantly lower than those for blue whales. Humpback whales are seen most frequently off central California during the fall, feeding primarily on krill.

Other cetaceans may also be seen in sanctuary waters. These include minke whales, Pacific white-sided dolphins, Risso's dolphins, northern right whale dolphin, common dolphins, killer whales, Dall's porpoises, harbor porpoises, bottlenose dolphins and beaked whales. Recent sighting reports can be found online.[5]

Northern right whale dolphins. Photo credit: Steve Lonhart, NOAA Monterey Bay National Marine Sanctuary.

---

5   http://montereybay.noaa.gov/visitor/whalewatching/welcome.html

BOATING

Boaters should drive slowly near sensitive habitats, such as kelp forests and bird rookeries, to minimize disturbance. It is especially important to operate boats slowly in the area close to shore that is frequented by marine mammals and people. Boaters should stay clear of surfers, divers, swimmers, and kayakers. Motorized craft are prohibited in some areas. Harbors have speed limits, and California law limits speed to 5 mph (8 km/h) within 100 feet (30 meters) of a bather or within 200 feet (61 meters) of a beach. In parts of Santa Cruz County, speed is limited to 5 mph (8 km/h) within 900 feet (274 meters) of the beach.

Motor boat driving close to kelp canopy off Westcliff Drive in Santa Cruz. Photo credit: Becky Stamski, Monterey Bay National Marine Sanctuary.

Except within the five designated zones and access routes,[6] operation of motorized personal watercraft in Zone 5 at Pillar Point is allowed only when a High Surf Warning is in effect for San Mateo County in December, January or February. A motorized personal watercraft is any vessel propelled by machinery and operated by standing on, sitting, kneeling astride or behind the vessel (instead of standing or sitting inside); or is less than 20 feet (6 meters) long and exempted from compliance with the U.S. Coast Guard's Maximum Capacities Marking for Load Capacity regulation; or is less than 20 feet (6 meters) long and propelled by a water jet pump or drive.

KAYAKING

The Monterey Bay National Marine Sanctuary protects one of the world's most unique habitats: the giant kelp forest. These towering undersea forests are home to many fishes, invertebrates, birds, and marine mammals. Kayakers floating quietly in a kelp bed should watch for snails, crabs, and other small animals living on the kelp blades. They might even see a young rockfish hiding in the kelp canopy. Its cryptic coloration provides protection from predators as it hides among the broad kelp blades. The rockfish will move into deeper water as it grows older and larger.

Kayakers at San Carlos Beach explore a kelp bed overwhelmed by thousands of jellies. Photo credit: Steve Lonhart, NOAA Monterey Bay National Marine Sanctuary.

Paddling through the kelp forest, visitors may see brown pelicans, cormorants, loons, grebes, and other fish-eating birds that search the kelp forest for prey. Even sea gulls are common visitors to the kelp forest; they are often seen near sea otters, waiting to grab a few tidbits the otter may drop while eating. Kayakers will likely see seals, sea lions, or sea otters

---

6   http://montereybay.noaa.gov/intro/mp/032409summary_regs.pdf

in the sanctuary. Curious animals may even swim up to boats. Sea otters must rest about half the day to stay healthy. Each time a sleeping otter is disturbed, it wakes up, rolls in the water, and wets its fur. After this, otters must groom themselves and dry off before going back to sleep. Otter mothers and pups need more rest time than other animals. Kayakers are reminded to observe animals from a distance.

Marine mammals are protected by federal law. If they start to look in at people and fidget, that indicates that the people are much too close and should quietly back away. The National Oceanic and Atmospheric Administration (NOAA) recommends that people stay 50 to 100 yards (46–91 meters) away from all animals, whether in the water or on shore. In addition, sanctuary visitors should not feed marine mammals. It could be dangerous to the person, and is not healthy for the animals.

Kayakers staying well away from frolicking California sea lions. Photo credit: Steve Lonhart, NOAA Monterey Bay National Marine Sanctuary.

The Monterey Bay National Marine Sanctuary website provides a list of several kayak launch areas within the sanctuary.[7] Hazardous sea conditions may exist, especially at open beaches. Visitors should check with local kayak shops for current ocean conditions and should consider the skill limits of their group when planning a kayak trip. Kayakers should be aware of changing weather, which might include fog, wind, strong currents, and large surf. Suggested safety equipment includes a lifejacket, pump, paddle float, wet-quit, flotation bags for decked boats, and a safety kit.

---

7   http://montereybay.noaa.gov/visitor/kayak.html

DIVING/SNORKELING

With 6,094 square miles (15,783 km²) of water and 276 miles (442 km) of coastline there is no shortage of areas to snorkel or dive in the Monterey Bay National Marine Sanctuary. As divers or snorkelers slip under the surface of the water, they can glide through stunning kelp forests, home to many species of fish, sea stars, urchins, and nudibranchs and may be approached by a curious sea otter, harbor seal or sea lion.

Divers in the Monterey Bay National Marine Sanctuary can expect to find reefs and kelp forests abundant with fishes and marine invertebrates. Photo credit: Matthew Ferraro, Ocean Futures Society.

The sanctuary boasts some of the most popular dive spots in central and northern California, including the Breakwater in Monterey, Lovers Point in Pacific Grove, the Pinnacles at Carmel Bay and Whaler's Cove in Point Lobos State Park. Visibility varies from site to site, but averages 20 to 30 feet (6–9 meters) most of the year, with peaks of 60 feet (18 meters) from September to November. Water temperatures average in the mid-50°F (12–13°C) range year-round, with temperatures dropping into the 40s (8–9°C) at deeper sites.

Carmel River State Beach is a favorite launching spot for divers exploring the underwater kelp forests just offshore. Upwelling from the Carmel Submarine Canyon supplies nutrients for the abundant marine life in the area. However, the deep underwater canyon also contributes to dangerous surf conditions. The safest diving access is either from the north end of the beach near a rocky area or at the extreme south. The middle section is too steep for safe access.

Chad King, SIMoN GIS specialist, prepares to dive in Whaler's Cove at Point Lobos State Park. Photo credit: Steve Lonhart, NOAA Monterey Bay National Marine Sanctuary.

BEACH ACTIVITIES

There are 25 public beaches within the Monterey Bay National Marine Sanctuary. Picnicking, kite flying, surfing, tide pool exploration and surf fishing are popular activities. Some beaches allow campfires, and many allow dogs—however dogs must usually be on a leash.

People playing in waves on Salinas River State Beach, Moss Landing.
Photo credit: Becky Stamski, Monterey Bay National Marine Sanctuary.

A mile (1.6 km) offshore of Half Moon Bay State Beach is Maverick's, a famed big wave surfing spot. Winter storm surge waves can reach up to 20 feet (6 meters) high and are not recommended for novice surfers.

Two surfers take off on a large wave at Maverick's.
Photo credit: Josh Pederson, Monterey Bay National Marine Sanctuary.

The mile (1.6 km)-long sandy Santa Cruz Beach is a favorite of swimmers and is the location for many beach related activities, including professional competitions for beach volleyball. The Boardwalk was one of the first amusement parks constructed on a beach and is still popular with fun seekers of all ages. The Big Dipper is on the National Historic Record as one of the original wooden roller coasters still in existence. One of the newest attractions is a Haunted House in operation around Halloween.

Boardwalk rides, wharf and beach in Santa Cruz.
Photo credit: Becky Stamski, Monterey Bay National Marine Sanctuary.

AVIATION

Because of the potential disturbance to marine mammals and other wildlife, flying motorized aircraft below 1,000 feet (305 meters) above sea level in any of the four restricted zones[8] is prohibited.

---

8   http://montereybay.noaa.gov/intro/mp/032409summary_regs.pdf

Gulf of the Farallones

About the Gulf of the Farallones National Marine Sanctuary

The rocky pinnacles known as the Farallon Islands lie 27 miles (43 km) due west of the Golden Gate Bridge, at the entrance to San Francisco Bay. As part of America's National Wildlife Refuge system, they are uninhabited except for a small team of determined biologists that have studied and monitored the abundance of life on shore and under the sea for nearly forty years. The islands are surrounded by the Gulf of the Farallones National Marine Sanctuary, whose waters provide food and homes to an incredible diversity of marine life.

Southeast Farallon Island and West End Island, aerial photo. Photo credit: Jan Roletto, NOAA.

It's no accident that life flourishes here. Underwater geography and currents create a phenomenon known as upwelling: the movement of deep, cold, nutrient-rich waters towards the sea's surface, which in turn supports one of the most productive fisheries in the world. Seabirds and other species that forage on rockfish, salmon and herring flock to the Gulf of the Farallones. And 36 different species of marine mammals join them, from the planet's largest giant, the blue whale, to the endangered northern fur seal.

The Gulf of the Farallones National Marine Sanctuary (GFNMS) spans 1,279-square-miles (3,313 km²) just north and west of San Francisco Bay, and protects open ocean habitats, nearshore tidal flats, rocky intertidal areas, estuarine wetlands, subtidal reefs, and coastal beaches within its boundaries. In addition, GFNMS has administrative jurisdiction over the northern portion of the Monterey Bay National Marine Sanctuary, from the San Mateo/Santa Cruz County line northward to the existing boundary between the two sanctuaries and maintains offices in both San Francisco and Half Moon Bay.

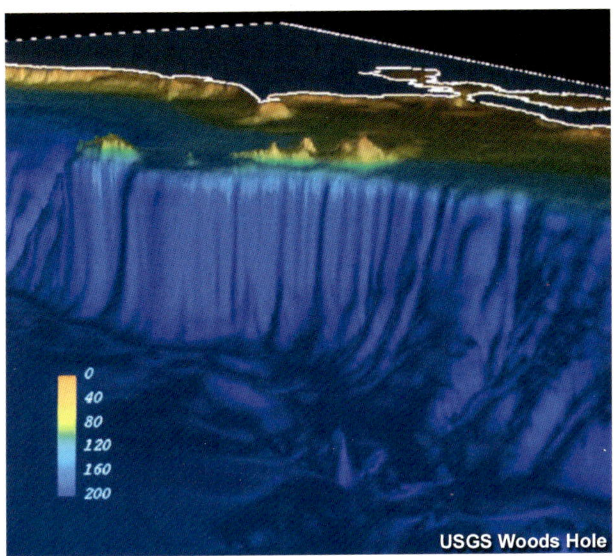

Computer imagery shows the topography of the seafloor of the Gulf of the Farallones National Marine Sanctuary, and the steep drop-off of the continental slope past the Farallon Islands. Image credit: USGS Woods Hole.

GFNMS is located within the California Current ecosystem, one of four major eastern boundary currents in the world, stretching along the western coast of North America from southern Canada to northern Mexico. Because of a high degree of wind-driven upwelling, there is a ready supply of nutrients to surface waters and the California Current ecosystem is one of the most biologically productive regions in the world. GFNMS is a globally significant, extraordinarily diverse, and productive marine ecosystem that supports abundant wildlife and valuable fisheries.

Why a National Marine Sanctuary?

The sanctuary was designated in 1981 because its waters provide important marine and nearshore habitats for a diverse array of marine mammals and birds in addition to fishery, plant, algal and benthic resources. The Gulf of the Farallones is a complex region with high biological diversity; nationally significant wildlife breeding and foraging areas; significant commercial and recreational fishing; estuarine habitats; numerous federally, state and locally protected marine and estuarine waters; watershed influences and impacts from eight million San Francisco Bay Area residents.

Fishermen stand in the surf at Ocean Beach in San Francisco to bring home the bounty. Photo credit: Gulf of the Farallones National Marine Sanctuary.

The sanctuary provides breeding and feeding grounds for at least twenty-five endangered or threatened species; thirty-six marine mammal species, including blue, gray, and humpback whales, harbor seals, elephant seals, Pacific white-sided dolphins, and one of the last populations of threatened Steller sea lions; over a quarter-million breeding seabirds; and one of the most significant white shark populations on the planet.

Hunted almost to extinction before being protected, the endangered blue whale is the largest creature to have ever lived on earth. Photo credit: Jim Knowlton, Ocean Futures Society.

The sanctuary illustrates how important the ocean and its wildlife and habitats are for the economic and social well-being of the region:

- The gulf region has supported large commercial fisheries, including a large percentage of the San Francisco fleet. Dungeness crab, salmon and groundfish (such as sanddab and California halibut) are the top fisheries in the gulf region.
- Sport fishing also generates revenue for the party boat fleets operating out of Bodega Bay, San Francisco and Half Moon Bay.
- Whale watching and offshore excursions are other activities that have grown in popularity.
- The sanctuary contains some of the West Coast's busiest shipping lanes.

Managing an area with such a rich abundance and diversity of marine life near the bustling San Francisco Bay area brings a great number of challenges. Water quality, habitat destruction through development, wildlife disturbance, invasive species and other issues must be continually evaluated and addressed. The sanctuary partners with many agencies, organizations and individuals to protect, study, manage and teach about this precious resource.

Golden Gate Bridge at sunrise. Photo credit: Carrie Vonderhaar, Ocean Futures Society.

Resources within the Gulf of the Farallones National Marine Sanctuary

The sanctuary contains a complex system of bays, estuaries, mudflats, marsh and intertidal, coastal and oceanic waters.

ROCKY SHORES

The rocky shores of the Gulf of the Farallones National Marine Sanctuary support an extraordinarily rich array of algae and animals. In fact, more than 320 invertebrate species and 250 algal species have been identified along the sanctuary's rocky shores, which are divided into a series of zones that are defined by the amount of time the rocks are exposed to air and water. Different algal and invertebrate species inhabit each of these zones.

The Sanctuary meets the land with force in the rocky intertidal zone. High energy waves are often present along shoreline areas of the Gulf of the Farallones. Photo credit: Dan Howard, NOAA.

- *The Splash Zone*

  Few species have adaptations to survive in the splash zone. Organisms that survive here are almost always exposed to the air and are rarely submerged by water. Marine invertebrates such as periwinkle snails, barnacles, limpets and a type of green algae are among the few species that can survive here.

- *The High Zone*

  Organisms that inhabit this zone are exposed to air for about 72 percent of the time. The lined shore crab survives in this zone by positioning its flat body in rock crevices, out of direct sunlight and hidden from larger predators. Limpets, chitons and black turban snails form a watertight seal onto the rocks with their shells to protect themselves from desiccation (drying out). Some algal species, such as rockweed, have moisture-retention adaptations that enable them to survive for many hours exposed to sunlight and air.

The rocky intertidal comprises a narrow ribbon of habitat along the coast of the Gulf of the Farallones. Many species of invertebrates and algae thrive in this unique habitat which is exposed and submerged twice a day. Photo credit: Joe Heath, NOAA.

- *The Mid Zone*

  The mid zone is marked by a high density of living organisms. Black turban snails and aggregating anemones are common here. The California mussel also occupies this zone and can form large beds that provide important refuge and habitat for a variety of invertebrates and algae.

- *The Low Zone*

  In this zone, organisms may be exposed to air just a few times a month. Species that survive here are more resilient to waves and less resilient to air exposure. The giant green anemone, the purple sea urchin and the sunflower star are invertebrates that frequent the sanctuary's lower intertidal and subtidal regions. The sea palm, a beautiful and edible alga, is also common in the exposed low zones of the sanctuary's rocky shores.

Sea palms exposed at low tide. Photo credit: Maia McGuire.

BEACHES

Sandy beaches form a small but important part of the Gulf of the Farallones National Marine Sanctuary coastline. Sandy shores in Marin and San Francisco Counties are characterized mainly by relatively short stretches of sandy beach and several pocket beaches—a marked contrast with many areas to the south, such as the shoreline of Monterey Bay. Most beaches here are characterized by medium- and fine-grained sand. Popular beaches along the Gulf's oceanic shores include Stinson and Muir. In addition to these, sandy beaches exist along Tomales Bay; some of the more popular ones there include Brazil and Tomasini.

Sunrise at Stinson Beach in Marin County is a sight to behold in the early glow of morning. Twenty minutes from San Francisco, this is a popular weekend destination. Photo credit: Patty Gaffney, NOAA.

CONTINENTAL SHELF

The continental shelf is characterized by gently dipping seafloor and forms a relatively flat surface (hence the name, "shelf") compared to the steeper and deeper continental slope. It extends nearly 35 miles (50 kilometers) in the gulf region – wider than in areas to the north and south of the sanctuary – and provides an especially large, relatively shallow habitat for foraging coastal and oceanic seabirds, marine mammals and fishes. The greatest water depth is less than approximately 500 feet (150 meters).

The shelf seafloor in the sanctuary consists mostly of continuously-shifting sediment (sand, silt and minor amounts of broken shell material) along with areas of rock outcrops and coarse gravel. The most notable seafloor features are the large underwater sand dunes between the Farallon Islands and Point Reyes and the approximately 11-mile (18-kilometer)-long rocky ridge that includes Hurst Shoal, Farallon Islands, Fanny Shoals, Rittenberg Bank and Noonday Rock.

Sea pens. Photo credit: Claire Fackler, NOAA National Marine Sanctuaries.

Along with clams, dense fields of sea pens are found on the silty shelf. Each sea pen is a colony of polyps (small anemone-like individuals) that is anchored to the soft-sediment bottom and visually resembles old-fashioned quill pens.

Dungeness crabs, one of the most economically important fisheries in the area, are concentrated on sandy and silty seafloor areas. They are opportunistic feeders, consuming clams, fishes, isopods and amphipods.

Dungeness crabs are common in the Gulf of the Farallones and are a favorite menu item.
Photo credit: Gulf of the Farallones National Marine Sanctuary.

Flatfishes, such as California halibut and sanddabs, use the sandy seafloor to evade predators and conceal themselves from prey by burying themselves up to their eyes.

The complex physical structure created by rocky, hard-bottom areas within the outer continental shelf region provides habitats for a very different suite of organisms than those found in soft-bottom areas: rockfishes, deep-water corals, sponges, anemones and others. This abundance of benthic life associated with hard substrates attracts pelagic predators, including seabirds and marine mammals, which hunt for fish and invertebrate prey along the bottom and in the waters above the seafloor.

Fabien Cousteau studies urchins, sea stars and anemones at the Farallon Islands.
Photo credit: Carrie Vonderhaar, Ocean Futures Society.

ESTUARIES

Estuaries are places where fresh and salt water mix. They support highly diverse communities and provide crucial links to many nearby ecosystems. Marine mammals and seabirds living on the Farallon Islands and the mainland coast depend as much on the integrity and productivity of these estuarine waters and adjacent ocean as on the preservation of the shore areas they use for breeding, feeding and hauling out (coming ashore).

The Estero de San Antonio and the Estero Americano are unique brackish rivers that are within the Gulf of the Farallones National Marine Sanctuary. Photo credit: Dan Howard, NOAA.

The Gulf of the Farallones National Marine Sanctuary encompasses four major estuaries: Tomales Bay, Bolinas Lagoon, Estero Americano and Estero de San Antonio. These estuaries provide important marine and nearshore habitats for a diverse array of marine mammals and birds in addition to fishery, plant, algal and benthic resources. They are also important components of the Pacific Flyway, one of the four principal bird migration routes in North America.

The picturesque wetlands of Tomales Bay stretch inshore and provide important habitat for birds on the Pacific flyway. Photo credit: Dan Howard, NOAA.

Large numbers of marine mammal enthusiasts and bird-watchers spend time along the sanctuary's coastal estuaries and shorelines observing marine mammals, shorebirds, waders and waterfowl. Some of the most popular places to see seals and other wildlife are within the sanctuary estuaries, such as Tomales Bay and Bolinas Lagoon, as well as within the adjacent Point Reyes National Seashore at Drakes and Limantour Esteros. There is a resident harbor seal population that breeds in Tomales Bay. The seal population ranges between 500 and 800 seals depending on the time of year.

Harbor seals haul out on algae-covered rocks. Photo credit: Carrie Vonderhaar, Ocean Futures Society.

Tomales Bay and Bolinas Lagoon sit on top of the San Andreas Fault and are submerged linear estuaries that run along the plate boundaries. Phytoplankton is the primary vegetation in the open-water portion of these habitats, and eelgrass is commonly found in tidal and upper subtidal zones of Tomales Bay and the Esteros.

Eelgrass plays an important role within the estuaries. More than 20,000 shorebirds and seabirds—including loons, grebes, geese, cormorants and ducks—winter in Tomales Bay; these migratory birds feed upon the abundant fish and invertebrate species associated with the eelgrass beds. Pacific herring use the beds for spawning. Eelgrass also supports a diverse invertebrate community, including snails, shrimp, nudibranchs and sea hares. The beds also help trap sediments and reduce excess nutrients and pollutants in the water column, and they serve as buffer zones, protecting the coast from erosion.

Taylor's sea hare in eelgrass bed. Photo credit: Jennifer Stock/Cordell Bank National Marine Sanctuary.

Fish species found in the Esteros include Pacific herring, staghorn sculpin and starry flounder. The endangered tidewater goby breeds in the shallow waters of Estero de San Antonio. Tomales Bay supports seasonal populations of salmon, steelhead, sardine and lingcod, which are important local fisheries. Leopard sharks breed in Tomales Bay. The shallow bay's sandy bottom attracts a variety of bottom-dwelling fishes including sole, halibut, skates and rays. White sharks hunt for seals and sea lions that haul out on the sandy beaches and rocks near the mouth of Tomales Bay.

Lingcod. Photo credit: Brian Hall, Ocean Futures Society .

Sea otters are extremely rare in these waters, however, river otters are observed occasionally in Tomales Bay headwaters. The rapid disappearance of this habitat, undergoing conversion for agriculture and aquaculture, poses a particular threat to these vulnerable species.

The soft-bottom habitats support large concentrations of burrowing organisms, such as clams, snails, worms and crabs.

ROCKY ISLANDS

The Farallon Islands, the most prominent islands in the sanctuary, provide important breeding and resting sites for many of the marine birds and mammals that migrate through the sanctuary. In addition, there are a number of coastal rocks and islets within the sanctuary, such as Bird Rock (near Tomales Point), Double Point and Point Resistance rocks (near Point Reyes) that are important breeding and resting sites.

The sanctuary manages the marine environment below the mean high tide line for all exposed rocks and islands within its boundaries. At the Farallon Islands, land above the mean high tide line constitutes the Farallon National Wildlife Refuge and is managed by the US Fish and Wildlife Service. The Farallones consist of seven islands that are part of a granite ridge that rises along the seafloor at the western edge of the continental shelf and lie within one of the largest upwelling centers in the world.

Farallon Islands, aka "The Devil's Teeth", 27 miles due west of San Francisco, California.
Photo credit: Carrie Vonderhaar, Ocean Futures Society.

OPEN OCEAN

The open ocean is a vast place. It is essentially bottomless and without sides – an endless column of water. As such, it requires special adaptations for survival: animals in this realm are either "drifters" or swift "swimmers."

Drifters include the larvae of many fishes and invertebrates as well as larger organisms like jellies, salps, krill and copepods.

Comb jellies are nearly transparent. However, when illuminated, their fringing cilia (tiny hairs used for limited swimming) dance with the all the colors of the rainbow. Photo credit: Dr. Richard C. Murphy, Ocean Futures Society.

Rather than floating with the currents, **swimmers**—such as fishes, turtles, oceanic dolphins, migrating pinnipeds and whales—are capable of moving against currents and making prolonged migrations that may be unrelated to ocean currents.

Some open-ocean creatures (such as many of the jellies and other gelatinous organisms) are transparent, or nearly so. By contrast, many fishes and marine mammals use counter-shading, well illustrated by the great white shark. These animals are darker on top and lighter on the bottom. This allows them to blend in to the background: to an organism looking down on the shark, its dark upper body blends into the dark waters below; likewise, from underneath, the shark's light underbelly blends into the waters lit from above.

The white underside of the white shark and its grey upper body provide camouflage called counter-shading. Photo credit: Bob Wilson, Gulf of the Farallones National Marine Sanctuary.

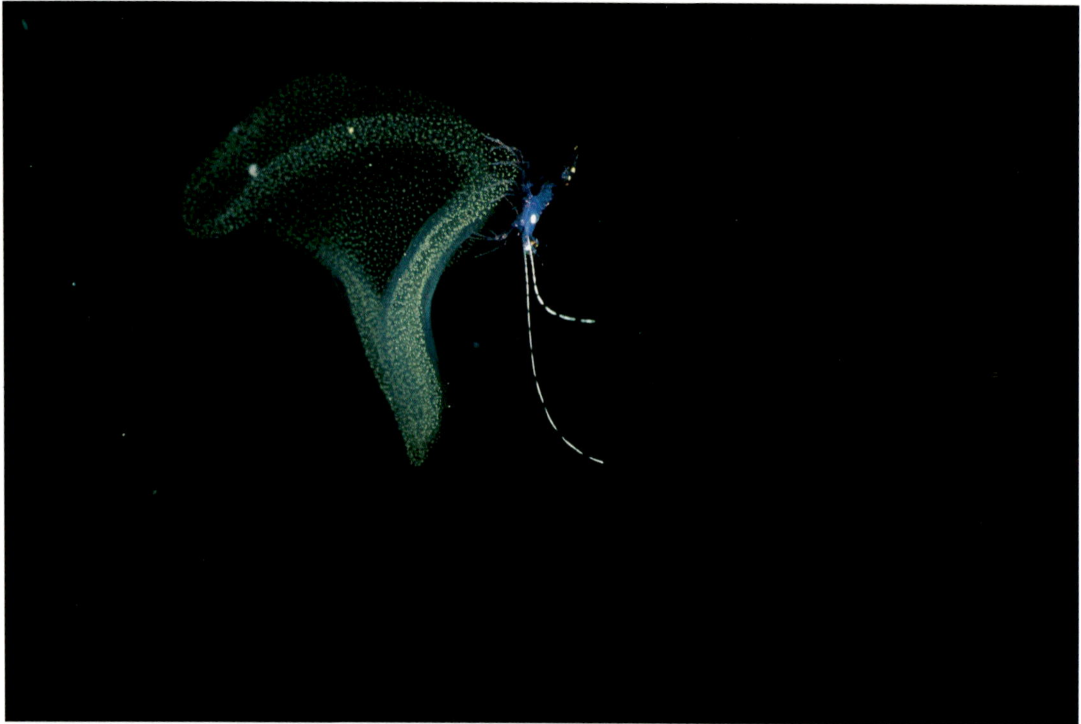

Zooplankton. Photo credit: Dr. Richard C. Murphy, Ocean Futures Society.

The open-ocean habitat in the sanctuary is strongly influenced by the oceanographic patterns of the northern California coast. Strong upwelling events stimulate the productivity of organisms at all levels of the marine food web. Cool, nutrient-rich, upwelled waters support high primary productivity. The sanctuary is situated in one of only five coastal upwelling zones in the world, and while these regions together constitute only about one percent of the total area of the ocean, they have been estimated to supply some 50 percent of the world's commercial fish catches. Upwelling enhances primary production in these areas, making them 'hotspots' for marine life.

Copepod with eggs. Photo credit: Matt Wilson/Jay Clark, NOAA NMFS AFSC.

In upwelling regions like the Gulf of the Farallones, the zooplankton is dominated by copepods and krill. Copepods are small crustaceans that are less than a tenth of an inch (1–2 mm) long. They spend their entire lives as tiny zooplankton, drifting with ocean currents and serving as food for other invertebrates and fishes. Arguably the most important group of crustaceans, these one-eyed arthropods make up more than 70 percent of the zooplankton in the open ocean.

Much larger than their copepod cousins, krill are shrimp-like crustaceans that are approximately a half inch to two inches (1.25 to five centimeters) in length. They are omnivores, feeding in particular on phytoplankton, copepods and even fish larvae; in turn, they are eaten by many predators, including salmon, seabirds and marine mammals.

DEEP SEA HABITAT

In the deep waters of the Gulf of the Farallones National Marine Sanctuary lie unique organisms and dramatic geological features. Less than 50 miles (80 kilometers) offshore, the steep continental slope descends into the deep sea to depths beyond 660 feet (200 meters) with the deepest parts of the sanctuary exceeding 6,500 feet (2,000 meters).

The deep sea is the largest habitat on earth and is home to many relatively unknown biological communities. It is only in the past two decades that better technologies have allowed humans to view previously unseen areas: the development of camera-equipped remotely-operated vehicles (ROVs) and manned submersibles provide a new window on this world.

The KRAKEN II, remotely-operated vehicle (ROV) from University of Connecticut.
Photo credit: Kaitlin Graff, NOAA.

There are two major habitats in the deep sea:

The midwater: Animals such as fishes, squid and jellies live their entire lives floating here, in the vast area where one can see neither the seafloor below nor the sunlight above. Small bacteria and crustaceans are also abundant in this zone.

Midwater squid. Photo credit: MBARI.

The seafloor, or benthos: This habitat is dominated by microscopic animals living in the mud, a diverse array of larger surface-dwelling invertebrates (sea stars, urchins, sponges, brittle stars, etc.) and fishes that live on or just above the seafloor.

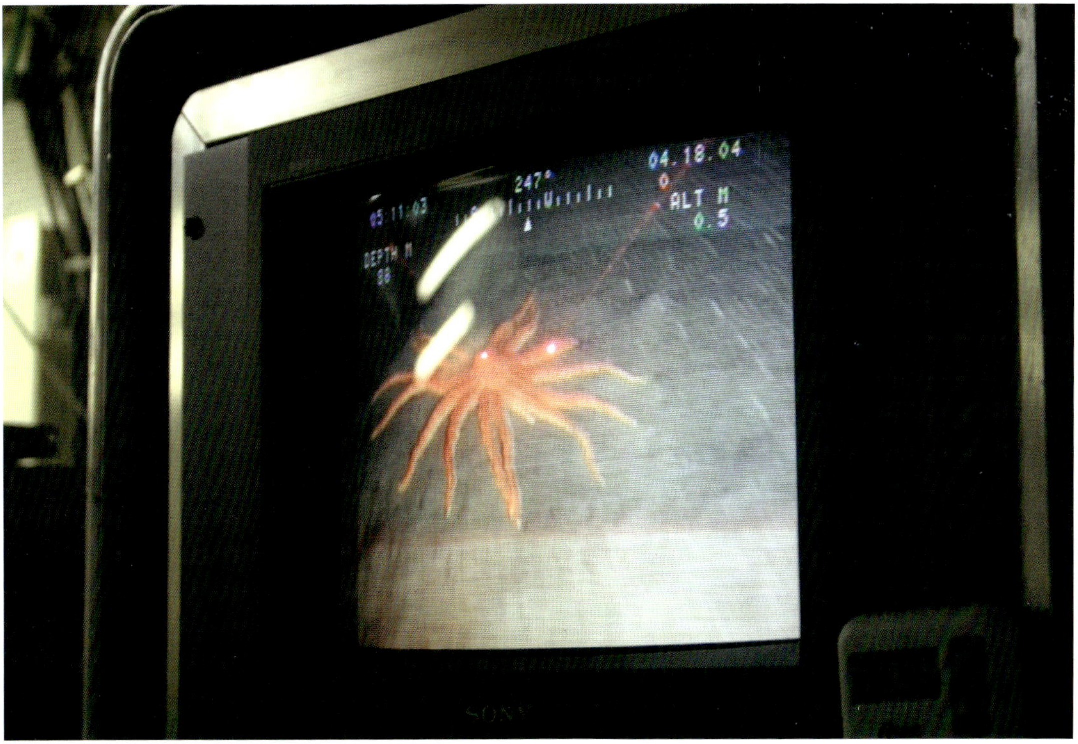

Live video from the seafloor aboard the R/V McArthur II. Photo credit; Chad King, SIMoN/NOAA.

Deep-sea life is adapted to dark, cold, high-pressure and low-oxygen conditions. Compared to the relatively shallow water habitats (less than 650 feet/200 meters) along the California coast, food is generally scarce at depth. Some animals adjust to these harsh conditions, making use of a habitat few others can tolerate; it reduces competition for food and their chances of being eaten.

Organisms have adapted in a variety of ways. Natural light penetrates to only about 1000 feet (300 meters), so marine plants, which need sunlight, are absent below this depth. Because it is dark, many animals don't have the ability to see; others have extraordinarily sensitive eyes to pick up what little light is available. Many deep-sea organisms make their own light—a chemical reaction called bioluminescence. Bright displays of light may be used to communicate, attract mates, create confusion (and thus avoid a predator) or lure food.

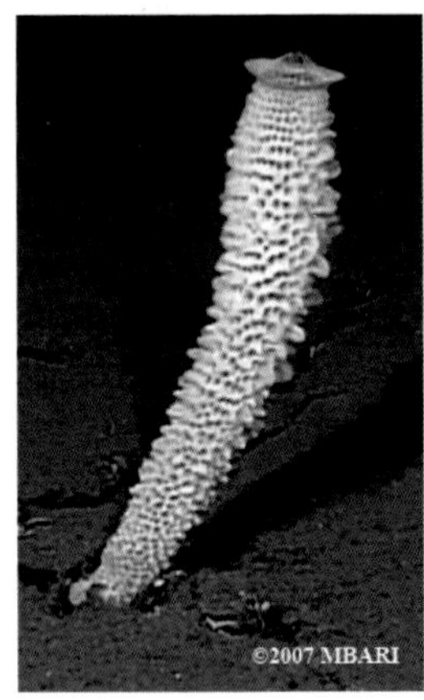

Glass sponge.
Photo credit: MBARI.

The cold water slows an animal's metabolism. Most deep-sea animals move very slowly, and some employ special enzymes to deal with this unique environment. Slow metabolism may account for the long lives of deep-sea organisms, including certain rockfishes that can live for more than 200 years. Other animals, like sea cucumbers, carry high levels of unsaturated fat in their cell walls to maintain membrane fluidity in this cold, high-pressure environment.

Food is generally limited in the deep sea, so finding it and capturing it is more difficult. Many animals feed on an array of discarded biological material called "detritus," which rains down from above as a result of the activities of animals in shallower water. Whatever these animals discard or shed provides food that sinks to the seafloor for scavengers and mud-feeding organisms like brittle stars and sea cucumbers. On occasion, large "food falls," like dead whales or dead kelp, sink from above, attracting large numbers of animals that come to take advantage of the bounty.

Deep ocean urchin and crab. Photo credit: MBARI.

NATIVE PEOPLE

The Coast Miwok, the first peoples near San Francisco, are part of the cultural heritage of the Gulf of the Farallones National Marine Sanctuary. Living in village communities, they built a strong culture based around fishing and gathering and hunting on land and sea. The ocean provided crabs, abalone, oysters and fish. They made flat beads from clam shells, which were strung together and used for trade throughout much of Northern California. While much of their culture has been lost, they regained federal recognition as a tribe in 2002 and there are some 500 Coast Miwok tribal members today.

Key Species within the Sanctuary

SEABIRDS AND SHOREBIRDS

One of the most spectacular components of the Gulf of the Farallones National Marine Sanctuary's abundant and diverse marine life is the populations of nesting and migratory seabirds: it hosts more than 300,000 breeding seabirds—the largest concentration in the contiguous United States. These birds are highly dependent on the sanctuary's productive waters.

Pigeon guillemots like this one nest on the Farallon Islands. Photo credit: Steve Lonhart, SIMoN/NOAA.

Thirteen bird species have breeding colonies on the Farallon Islands and feed in the sanctuary. More than 160 species use the sanctuary for shelter, food or as a migration corridor. Of these, 57 species are known to use the sanctuary during their breeding season. At least 19 marine and coastal bird species that are federally listed as threatened, endangered or a species of concern can be found here, including the marbled murrelet and the western snowy plover.

Endangered Western Snowy Plover. Photo credit: Laird Henkel, NOAA.

Education programs within the Gulf of the Farallones National Marine Sanctuary aim to reduce human threats to seabirds. Visitors are reminded that seabirds that nest and rest on cliffs or offshore rocks are sensitive to human disturbance. Disturbances to seabirds during breeding season can: scare birds off their nests; dislodge eggs and chicks from nest sites; allow predators access to eggs and chicks; lead to deaths when eggs and chicks are exposed to heat and cold or cause chicks to drown when they are forced to leave the nest too soon.

SALMON

Salmon spend their adult lives in the open ocean before returning to their native streams to spawn. They are called an *anadromous* species, meaning they begin their life in fresh water habitats before migrating to salt water environments. Salmon live in the ocean from one to seven years where they grow and become sexually mature. When the time comes to reproduce, they may use any number of cues ranging from currents, tides, temperature, and salinity gradients to identify their native river. During this return journey, some individuals can travel up to 3,000 miles (4,800 km). Once salmon reach their destination, the females create a nest (called a redd) and lay their eggs. The males then fertilize the eggs with sperm (called milt).

Chinook salmon.
Photo credit: NOAA NMFS.

Chinook and Coho salmon have only one chance to successfully spawn, because they die shortly after reproducing. Steelhead trout may survive to spawn several more times throughout their life. The fertilized eggs hatch after four to six weeks. Once the young emerge, they feed off a yolk sac and are called alevin. The yolk sac provides nutrients for two to three weeks, after which the alevin leave the redd to find food. After leaving the redd, the young salmon (called fry) eat insects and are vulnerable to predators. Dark bars along the sides of their bodies(called parr marks) help to camouflage the fry. During their journey migrating downstream to the ocean, they become larger and undergo physiological adaptations to live in the salt water through a process called smoltification. As a "smolt," their gills and kidneys adapt to saltier water, and their color becomes silvery. They also imprint the scent of their home stream in order to return years later to spawn.

Salmon smolt. Photo credit: NOAA.

Next, salmon travel through an estuary (an area where fresh water meets salt water). Most of the physiological changes occur in an estuary, where the fish may stay as long as six months. The San Francisco Bay, Bolinas Lagoon, and Tomales Bay are estuaries where young smolts can be found before they migrate into the sanctuary's waters.

Juvenile Chum or Dog Salmon. Photo credit: Carrie Vonderhaar, Ocean Futures Society.

From the moment the eggs hatch, young salmonids face endless predators and life obstacles. They are prey for other fish and birds. The large numbers of individuals hatched result in large numbers being eaten, as up to 80% of new alevin are lost. If they survive the migration to the ocean, they face additional predation by dolphins, seals, sea lions, sharks, and humans. Without salmonids, entire food webs may be affected because many predators would be deprived of an important food source.

Some of the human influences that affect salmonids include:

- Dams, which prevent water flow necessary for fish migrations
- Pesticides from agricultural runoff, which can pollute salmonid habitat and food sources
- Road construction along streams, which can cause landslides and erosion that decrease habitat
- Dredging, which can remove habitat and stir up silt, reducing visibility in the water
- Logging, which can reduce shade that is needed to keep streams cool and can contribute to stream side erosion
- Overfishing practices, which can reduce the population, making it difficult for salmonids to recover and sustain their population numbers over time.

The fishing community has suffered low catch rates and a closed salmon fishery. Photo credit: Mary Jane Schramm, NOAA.

WHITE SHARKS

Given the difficulty of studying white sharks, it's no surprise the ocean's largest predatory fish still remains vastly misunderstood. Mythologized from ancient art to modern film, their stout bodies, long narrow pectoral fins, and that distinctive high dorsal triangle define the unmistakable profile of a hunter who continues to hold a public's fear and fascination. They have been recorded to reach lengths of 21 feet (6.4 meters) and may weigh up to 4,800 pounds (2,177 kg). Powerful and stealthy, their fluid movements are the work of dense muscles that ring their trunk, tails and fins shaped like aircraft wings that thrust them through the sea. Their cryptic shading, charcoal backs and white bellies allow them to blend effortlessly into the sea if viewed from above or below. Hiding in plain sight, they rely on ambush tactics to hunt their prey.

White sharks are powerful predators. Photo credit: NOAA.

Like bluefin tuna and makos, white sharks have adapted to survive in temperate oceans by elevating their body temperature above the surrounding sea. This approximation of "warm-bloodedness" allows their muscles to work more efficiently in a cold ocan, but at a cost: they need high-energy meals. For mature white sharks, this usually means seals. The elephant seal rookery at the Farallon Islands is only one of three hotspots in California where scientists can predictably study white sharks and then, for only a limited window of time. It turns out that these predators always believed to be residents are, in fact, only seasonal visitors. Scientists using satellite tags are just beginning to piece together the mystery of white shark migrations. Tracking data is revealing that these sharks range farther and deeper than ever imagined. Each fall they return to the west coast of the United States and Mexico, staying only six months before departing for the eastern Pacific.

The Farallones and other elephant seal rookeries offer scientists a unique chance to combine field observations with remote tracking. And learning more about the secret lives of these predators will, scientists hope, move them out of the realm of science fiction and give us a deeper understanding of the importance of apex predators in ocean ecosystems.

White sharks hunt elephant seals off the Farallon Islands. Photo credit: Bob Wilson, Gulf of the Farallones National Marine Sanctuary.

Unique markings on white sharks' fins can be used to identify individuals.
Photo credit: University of California, Davis.

Fierce predatory instincts are displayed from birth by young sharks in the womb. It begins with a peculiar form of development in which the great white, like some other sharks, retain their embryonic young. During gestation, baby sharks feed on yolk sacs. But this source of nutrition is exhausted before the young are born and so shark mothers begin to release unfertilized eggs for the developing young to consume. With fully functional, miniature white shark mouths, the babies survive through oophagy until they are born. White sharks deliver only four to seven pups per litter, each 48 to 60 inches long, fully wired for survival on their own in the open ocean. While scientists are just beginning to understand the basics of their early development and where and when they mate and give birth, their reproduction remains a lingering mystery.

Ironically, we are learning that the ocean's most feared predator may also be its most vulnerable. White sharks are exceptionally susceptible to fishing pressures because they grow and mature slowly, and only give birth to small numbers of young every other year. Like other pelagic sharks, great whites must navigate a maze of longlines and driftnets in the open sea to complete their migrations to other parts of the world. And through DNA tests of dried market samples, we've learned even the white shark is not safe from a fishery that hacks off only fins and tosses the living animal, minus its ability to swim, back to the sea.

White shark. Photo credit: Bob Wilson, Gulf of the Farallones National Marine Sanctuary.

A white shark investigates a fake seal decoy used by UC Davis researchers. Photo credit: University of California, Davis.

The growing awareness of the importance of white sharks has led to their protection in many coastal waters around the world, but has also given rise to a public desire for personal encounters with real-life monsters of the sea. The increase in white shark dive operations since the 1990s pits field scientists against entrepreneurs at white shark feeding destinations like the Gulf of the Farallones. And at the core of the dilemma is the question: who has a right of access to the great whites and what do the sharks lose or gain?

White sharks inspire curiosity and awe among divers. Photo credit: Bob Wilson, Gulf of the Farallones National Marine Sanctuary.

"Does ecotourism affect sharks? It's a complicated question," Pete Klimley[1] explains when describing the interaction between tour boats and wildlife. "There is a potential to disrupt the normal feeding behavior because what happens is, the shark catches the seal, it dives under water carrying the seal until it loses all its blood and dies, and then it comes to the surface, and there's so much energy in that seal, [it's] such a valuable property that other sharks come in and a ritualized combat occurs. If this dining progression is prevented or altered, that's a potential problem."

---

1   Californian Dr. Pete Klimley began studying the Farallon sharks in 1987, and is one of the world's leading experts on shark behavior.

The Ocean Futures Society team members watch out for each other in the cold, murky waters of the Gulf of the Farallones National Marine Sanctuary. Photo credit: Carrie Vonderhaar, Ocean Futures Society

In August 1997, California Governor Pete Wilson signed a bill to give permanent protection to Great White Sharks in California waters—a marine conservation success made possible by 27 years of research from the Farallon Islands on this remarkable species. In March 2009, regulations went into effect prohibiting white shark attraction and approach in Gulf of the Farallones National Marine Sanctuary.

WHALES

The **gray whale** is the most common large cetacean seen from the shore. These baleen whales migrate annually from their feeding grounds in the Arctic Ocean and Bering Sea to the warm lagoons of Baja California (Mexico), where they give birth to their young.

Gray whale and calf. Photo credit: Wayne Perryman, Photogrammetry Program, NOAA SWFSC.

Gray whales migrate south through the Gulf of the Farallones beginning in November—with peak sightings during January and March. Males, newly impregnated females and juveniles come through from February through April, and females with their newborn calves follow along, from April through June. A few juveniles may appear in the gulf year-round off the Farallon Islands and in Bodega Bay.

Gray whales are primarily bottom feeders who power-shovel on their side for bottom-dwelling amphipods (crustacean-like organisms), krill and an occasional fish species such as herring.

A migrating humpback in the Farallones. Photo credit: NOAA Photo Library

Humpback whales are the most acrobatic of the baleen whales seen here. They use the gulf and Cordell Bank to the north as a feeding ground during the summer and fall months—feeding primarily over the continental shelf and slope break.

Lunges and surface thrusts are signs of surface feeding. Humpback prey consists primarily of planktonic shrimp, but they will also feed on schooling fishes such as herring, juvenile rockfishes and anchovy. Humpback whale distribution within the sanctuary is dependent on the distribution of prey species.

Blue whales, the largest animals ever to live on earth, migrate to the sanctuary during the late summer and are found here throughout the fall. The blue whale population seems to be increasing slowly.

At least 2,000 individual blue whales are found off the coast of California and Mexico. Their primary feeding grounds are in the Gulf of the Farallones, Cordell Bank and the Santa Barbara Channel. Their principal prey consists of krill.

Blue whale fluke. Photo credit: Josh Kaye-Carr, Channel Islands Naturalist Corps.

Emerging Environmental Issues

OIL SPILLS

Between 800 and 1,100 oil tankers enter San Francisco Bay each year. Because the major shipping lanes run through the Gulf of the Farallones National Marine Sanctuary, oil spills are a frequent occurrence there. Since 1984, six vessels have leaked a total of over 1.5 million gallons (5.7 million liters) of oil in the sanctuary. Oil spills pose a significant threat to the health and balance of life on the sanctuary's coast. Past spills, such as the 2007

Duxbury Reef at low tide. Photo credit: Ashley Smith, NOAA.

Cosco Busan oil spill in San Francisco Bay, have deposited oil on the sanctuary's rocky shores, including Duxbury Reef. Oil can smother mussel beds and kill acorn barnacles, limpets and other species. When oil coats fur-covered animals, such as fur seals and otters, or birds, it can prevent them from being able to use their fur or feathers to stay warm. Monitoring programs are vital in addressing the potential impacts, restoration and recovery rates from spills.

INVASIVE SPECIES

Introduced, invasive species can cause impacts to wildlife and habitats, decrease biodiversity and limit resiliency of wildlife and habitats to recover from anthropogenic impacts. Non-native invertebrates have made their way to the Gulf of the Farallones, many of them

Invasive green crab. Photo credit: Kerstin Wasson, NOAA/ESNERR.

via vessel ballast water discharge. To date, almost 150 species of introduced marine algae and animals have been identified in the sanctuary. Invasive invertebrates, such as the European green crab, make up more than 85 percent of all introductions in sanctuary waters. The green crab is a voracious predator. It feeds on bivalve mollusks like mussels, clams and oysters, as well as other crab species, such as Dungeness crabs. It also hosts a marine worm that can infect shore birds.

Research within the Sanctuary

Research projects within the sanctuary system help sanctuary managers to solve specific management problems, enhance ecosystem protection efforts, and assist in the interpretation of the ecosystem for the general public. Research and monitoring programs in the GFNMS include the following:

- Beach Watch: Trained citizen-scientists survey and document the resources of the sanctuaries. The program goals include creating a long-term data set of the birds and mammals using sanctuary beaches and early detection of natural or human-caused disturbances, such as oil spills.

- White Shark Stewardship Project: The goal of this project is to protect and conserve the white shark population that utilizes the sanctuary.

Beach Watch volunteers document the live and dead animals of the Sanctuary. Photo credit: Gulf of the Farallones National Marine Sanctuary.

Researchers photograph a white shark. Photo credit: Stanford University.

- Sanctuary Integrated Monitoring Network (SIMoN): The Gulf of the Farallones, Cordell Banks and Monterey Bay National Marine Sanctuaries all participate in SIMoN. The goals of SIMoN are to develop a database to track current and historic monitoring programs, integrate existing monitoring programs conducted in the sanctuary to provide a synoptic overview of this marine ecosystem, initiate basic surveys or characterizations of all sanctuary habitats and regions, establish a series of long-term monitoring efforts to fill in critical information gaps, initiate specific, question-driven monitoring efforts with fixed durations and provide timely and pertinent information to managers and decision makers, the research community, and the general public via a web site and other venues.

The landing where scientists and researchers arrive and depart the Farallon National Wildlife Refuge at the Farallon Islands. Photo credit: Carrie Vonderhaar, Ocean Futures Society.

Visiting the Sanctuary

Note: In the last section of the book, "When You Visit the Sanctuaries," is detailed information about resources found within each sanctuary to help visitors have an enjoyable and productive visit.

VISITOR'S CENTER

Gulf of the Farallones National Marine Sanctuary (Headquarters and Visitor's Center)
991 Marine Drive, The Presidio
San Francisco, CA 94129

Open Monday-Friday
10 a.m. – 4 p.m.
Admission: Educational programs are free. Donations are accepted, and are suggested for public programs. Public and school programs are by reservation only. Program offerings are described on the Visitor's Center Website.[2]
Telephone: 415-561-6622

Opened in 1978, this was the first visitor center in the National Marine Sanctuary Program. Visitors are invited to explore the visitor center located in the Old Coast Guard Station at Crissy Field in the Presidio of San Francisco. There they will be able to view the stunning 15-foot tall ocean murals on the walls, get their hands wet in the touch tank, discover the exciting adventures that await them in the sanctuary's waters, and learn how to get involved in protecting the marine environment. It is a great place to bring the kids and spend a day at the beach.

---

2   http://www.farallones.org/education/visitor_center.php

Curious kids and adults peer through the microscope exhibit in the Gulf of the Farallones National Marine Sanctuary Visitor Center in San Francisco, while grasping the importance of sanctuary science. Photo credit: Karina Racz, NOAA.

The Marine Sanctuary Visitor Center offers dozens of programs to introduce young people to the whales and white sharks, seabirds and seals, found just offshore. The Visitor Center is operated by sanctuary staff in partnership with the non-profit Marine Sanctuary Association.

ACTIVITIES

Activities in the Gulf of the Farallones National Marine Sanctuary include beachgoing, birdwatching, boating, exploring the coastside trail, fishing, kayaking, surfing, tidepooling and whale watching. The Farallones Marine Sanctuary Association offers links on its website that show locations for each of these activities.[3]

---

3   http://www.farallones.org/explore/index.php

BOATING

Boaters should be aware that, in order to protect the seagrasses, there are areas within Tomales Bay where anchoring is not permitted. More information about these restrictions can be found online.[4]

Motorized personal watercraft are prohibited within the sanctuary boundaries except for emergency use.

Kayaking the Estero de San Antonio is a rare opportunity for accessing one of the most remote reaches of the sanctuary. Photo credit: Maria Brown, NOAA.

---

4   http://farallones.noaa.gov/eco/tomales/tomales.html

DIVING

Hazardous conditions make waters in the Gulf of the Farallones National Marine Sanctuary unsuitable for diving.

FISHING

King salmon and rockfish have been the primary target species for sport fishing in the Gulf of the Farallones National Marine Sanctuary. Charter fishing trips are available from the San Francisco Bay area.

On some weekend days, more than 1,000 clam diggers harvest gaper, geoduck, Washington and littleneck clams. The tidal community includes a wide variety of invertebrates such as barnacles, limpets, black turban snails, mussels, sea anemones, abalone, and urchins, which may be harvested as well.

Vermilion rockfish. Photo credit: Chad King, SIMoN/NOAA.

Crevices and underhangs are home to black abalone and black turban snails.
Photo credit: Steve Lonhart, SIMoN/NOAA.

Management of commercial and recreational fisheries in California is the responsibility of the California Department of Fish and Game[5] in state waters (0–3 nautical miles/0–3.5 miles/0–5.6 km), and National Oceanic and Atmospheric Administration Fisheries[6] in federal waters (3–200 miles/5–320 km).

---

5   http://www.dfg.ca.gov
6   http://www.nwr.noaa.gov

Cordell Bank National Marine Sanctuary

About the Cordell Bank National Marine Sanctuary

The most remote of the five West Coast sanctuaries is Cordell Bank National Marine Sanctuary. Located 52 miles (83 km) northwest of the Golden Gate Bridge in northern California, this sanctuary is just north of the Gulf of the Farallones. Designated in 1989, the sanctuary protects 529 square miles (1370 km²) of ocean around Cordell Bank—a four-and-a-half mile (7.2 km) by nine-and-a-half mile (15.2 km) underwater mountain that rises to within 115 feet (35 meters) of the surface. The bank sits 22 miles (35 km) west of Point Reyes on the edge of the continental shelf, where the seafloor drops off precipitously into the depths.

Far offshore, in the midst of the California Current, Cordell Bank is a challenge to reach by boat, even on the best days. Approaching Cordell Bank by boat, a keen observer may become aware of little signs that announce the proximity of the underwater island below. The water is slightly greener and the activity of life, seals, sea lions, cetaceans, and dozens of species of birds, is immediately more pronounced.

Point Reyes, California, at sunset. Photo credit: Carrie Vonderhaar, Ocean Futures Society.

Cordell Bank falls within the California Current ecosystem, one of four major eastern boundary currents in the world. Coastal upwelling, a process associated with eastern boundary currents, initiates an annual productivity cycle at Cordell Bank that supports a rich biological community that includes local species as well as migratory sea turtles, fishes, seabirds and marine mammals that travel up to thousands of miles to feed around the bank. The combination of a healthy benthic community on the bank and its close proximity to offshore, open water species contributes to the unique biological diversity in a relatively confined area around Cordell Bank.

Pacific white-sided dolphin jumping through the air. Photo credit: Jamie Hall, NOAA.

Salmon, tuna and other large predatory fish use the sanctuary seasonally. Over 20 species of marine mammals migrate from around the globe to feed in these productive waters, as do many species of seabirds—including migratory albatrosses, shearwaters and petrels.

Bullers Shearwater and other seabirds at Cordell Bank National Marine Sanctuary. Photo credit: Michael Carver, Cordell Bank National Marine Sanctuary.

Beneath the breaking waves of a dark and chilly ocean, they found a brilliant canvas of invertebrate life: anemones, sponges, hydrocorals, crabs, urchins, worms, snails, and sea stars, covering every inch of space. The waters were crowded with lingcod and thousands of varieties of rockfish: rosy, yellowtail, cowcod and bocaccio, and were dense with krill, a principal food for migrating blue and humpback whales. Upwelling and an increase in the supply of available food are the reasons life flourishes and envelops the rocky pinnacles of Cordell Bank's submerged 4.5 mile by 9.5-mile (7.2 by 15.2 km) granitic plateau.

Cowcod. Photo credit: Dave Murfin, NOAA.

GEOLOGIC HISTORY

The Cordell Bank National Marine Sanctuary is situated on the Pacific Plate and Cordell Bank is the most prominent geological feature of the sanctuary. The bedrock of Cordell Bank formed about 100 million years ago as part of the southern Sierra Nevada mountain range. In the last 33 million years, the Pacific Plate moved north, sheared off part of the North American plate and carried Cordell Bank to its present location west of Point Reyes. The bank continues to move north at a rate of about two inches (five centimeters) per year.

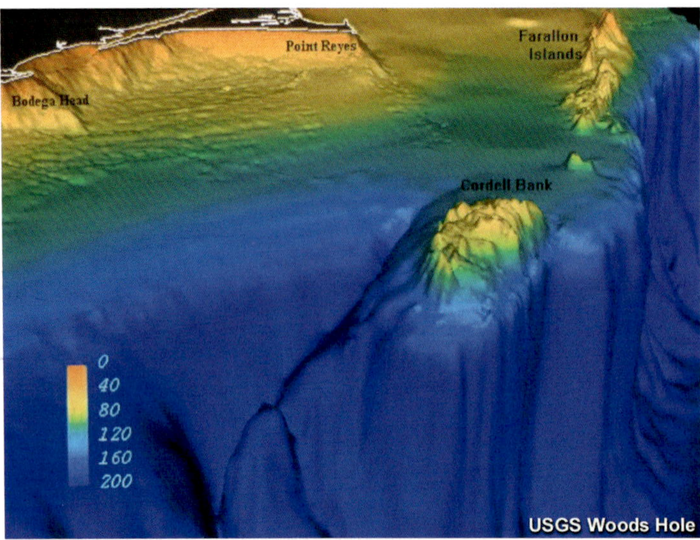

A computerized image of the topography of Cordell Bank.
Image credit: USGS Woods Hole.

Between 20,000 and 15,000 years ago, when sea level was about 360 feet (110 meters) below current sea level, most of Cordell Bank was exposed, making it a true island. Today, the sediments surrounding the base of Cordell Bank on the continental shelf are composed predominantly of silt and sand deposits that originated from rivers and coastal erosion.

Why a National Marine Sanctuary?

In the late 1800s there was a strong incentive to survey the coast of California to promote safer maritime commerce. Cordell Bank was discovered in 1853 by George Davidson of the U.S. Coast Survey while returning from a mapping expedition on California's north coast.

Edward Cordell, an accomplished surveyor, conducted additional surveys in 1869 when he was sent to relocate a "shoal west of Point Reyes." Cordell was attracted to the location by the numerous birds and marine mammals. To measure the depth, Cordell lowered a lead weight over the edge until it hit bottom and then measured the line on its return to the surface. Always considered a productive fishing area, not much was known about what life existed on the bank until 1977, when Cordell Bank was first explored underwater by a non-profit research association, Cordell Expeditions. Over the next 10 years, divers documented the organisms living on and above the bank. Through these efforts, images of the biological diversity of Cordell Bank were available to the public for the first time. This effort was instrumental in creating Cordell Bank National Marine Sanctuary, which was designated as the nation's eighth National Marine Sanctuary in 1989.

Ocean Futures Society's Matt Ferraro inspects the rich tapestry of sea life at Cordell Bank National Marine Sanctuary. Photo credit: Carrie Vonderhaar, Ocean Futures Society.

Managers of the Cordell Bank National Marine Sanctuary strive to protect the region's natural resources despite the diverse activities putting pressure on them. Fishing activity has been conducted at Cordell Bank since the late 1800s and commercial and recreational fishing are still major activities. Restrictions implemented by the Pacific Fisheries Management Council to help rebuild depleted rockfish stocks limit current fishing activity within the sanctuary. The southeast corner of Cordell Bank National Marine Sanctuary is located approximately six miles (9.6 km) from the terminus of the northern shipping lanes that funnel commercial vessels into and out of San Francisco Bay. On average, 2,000 large commercial ships transit through the sanctuary each year. There have been several large oil spills just south of the sanctuary in the last decade.

A common dolphin rides the bow wave. Photo credit: Carrie Vonderhaar, Ocean Futures Society.

Wildlife viewing trips are becoming increasingly popular in the sanctuary as opportunities to see humpback and blue whales and a diverse assemblage of pelagic seabirds draw enthusiasts from around the greater San Francisco Bay Area. Charter trips leave from the port of Bodega Bay.

Because of the offshore nature of the Cordell Bank sanctuary and the distance from major urban population centers, most water quality parameters suggest relatively good conditions. Benthic habitat quality has been impacted over the years as a result of bottom contact fishing gear on the rocky reef and soft bottom habitats of the sanctuary. Many derelict long lines and gill nets remain entangled on rocky areas of the bank. Fishing gear restrictions that are currently in place in some areas will help protect sanctuary habitats and conditions are expected to improve. Living resource conditions within Cordell Bank National Marine Sanctuary are considered to be diminished because of depleted populations of rockfish, salmon, leatherback sea turtles and some species of seabirds. It might be expected that conditions for living resources will improve due to fishery closures that are helping to rebuild depleted fish stocks, but uncertainty remains because of global changes that are currently affecting the ocean. To date, no maritime archaeological resources have been identified in the sanctuary.

The Mission Statement: "Cordell Bank National Marine Sanctuary's highest priority is resource protection. The Sanctuary takes a leading role in ecosystem management, focusing on natural and physical; processes. Together, with our partners, we work to protect biological communities, habitats, populations, and ecosystem dynamics. By addressing current management issues and anticipating future challenges to Cordell Bank, we strive to maintain a healthy marine environment for now and future generations."

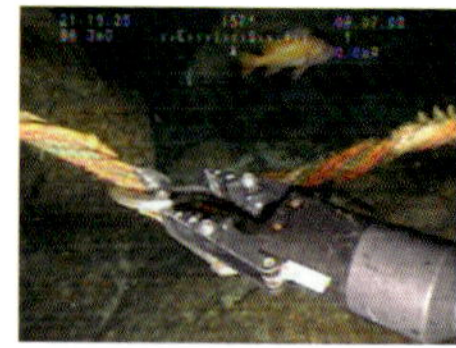

Using a remotely-operated vehicle (ROV) to remove fishing debris at Cordell Bank. Photo credit: Craig Bussel, Cordell Bank National Marine Sanctuary.

Resources within the Sanctuary

CONTINENTAL SHELF

The continental shelf is the gradually sloping submerged part of the continent that extends from the shore to the shelf break. The boundaries of Cordell Bank National Marine Sanctuary include only the outer continental shelf, with depths of approximately 230 to 656 feet (70 to 194 meters). The continental shelf makes up sixty-five percent of the sanctuary seafloor. A large portion (313 square miles/811 km^2) of the shelf in the sanctuary is composed of sand and mud bottoms. Soft bottom-associated species live either on the surface of, or buried in the sediments. Cordell Bank emerges from the soft sediments of the continental shelf at depths of 300 to 400 feet (91–122 meters) and reaches to within 115 feet (35 meters) of the ocean's surface.

Corals, anemones and sponges on Cordell Bank.
Photo credit: Richard Starr, Cordell Bank National Marine Sanctuary.

CONTINENTAL SLOPE

The continental slope makes up 190 square miles (500 km²) of the sanctuary (35% of the sanctuary seafloor) and extents from 656 feet (200 meters) down to 6,955 feet (2120 meters) at the western boundary of the sanctuary. The slope environment is primarily mud bottom with some rock habitats. Little is known about the slope region within this sanctuary; however, several research submersible dives have been conducted on the upper slope between 656 and 984 feet (200 and 300 meters). Fishes observed on the mud substrate include spotted ratfish, poachers, English sole, slender sole, stripetail rockfish, splitnosed rockfish, long-spined combfish, hagfish, and six-gilled shark. Aggregations of the fragile pink sea urchin are commonly observed on the mud bottom of the upper slope.

Pacific hagfish. Photo credit: Dave Murfin, NOAA.

SUBMARINE CANYONS

Several small submarine canyons cut into the continental slope of the sanctuary. These features are located west of the bank and extend to greater depths beyond the sanctuary's western boundary. The walls and floors of submarine canyons cover a small proportion of the Cordell Bank sanctuary seafloor. There is virtually no information on the habitats and biological communities within the submarine canyons located in the sanctuary. However, because submarine canyons extend from shallow waters of the continental shelf to the deep sea and contain a wide range of habitats, they contain an incredible diversity of organisms. The majority of canyon habitat is expected to be soft-bottom, while a much smaller portion is predicted to be hard-bottom.

Found in depths over 3000 feet, the spotted ratfish occasionally makes its way to shallower reefs and banks. Photo credit: Carrie Vonderhaar, Ocean Futures Society.

SEA MOUNTS AND BANKS

A bank is an elevation of the seafloor located on the continental shelf, over which the water depth is relatively shallow. These features are of continental origin and can cover extensive surface area but are not particularly high. By contrast, seamounts are mainly volcanic in origin, rise a considerable height from great depths on the continental rise and are limited in length across the summit.

Despite their differences in scale, both banks and seamounts are isolated in space and have higher elevation and a different substrate than the surrounding seabed. The vertical structure, habitat complexity and rocky substrate of banks and seamounts support a very different biological assemblage than the surrounding soft bottom typical of the continental shelf and slope. Because these rocky features extend up into the water column, they provide ideal habitat for attached sessile invertebrates that depend on currents to deliver their food. The hard substrate is also favorable for settlement of larvae from the water column.

A large group of yellowtail rockfish swims by a coral reef. Photo credit: Cordell Bank Expeditions.

The bathymetry and location of Cordell Bank combine to make it a very productive marine environment. The bank is situated downstream from a major and persistent upwelling center at Point Arena to the north. Nutrients and productivity emanating from that area are carried over the bank and sustain a thriving biological community. In addition to the Point Arena upwelling center, localized upwelling may also contribute to productivity at Cordell Bank.

The bank is located on the edge of an underwater peninsula and is surrounded by deep water on three sides. Within 7 miles (11 kilometers) of its western edge, the seafloor drops to 1.1 miles (1.8 km) at the sanctuary's western boundary. Data suggest that, as deeper water encounters the base of the bank on the northern edge, the water mass moves up and over the bank. This localized upwelling would be one more mechanism delivering food and nutrients to organisms living on or around Cordell Bank.

Rockfish, sponges, coral and anemone at Cordell Bank.
Photo credit: Richard Starr, Cordell Bank National Marine Sanctuary.

A rich blanket of pink strawberry anemones carpets Cordell Bank.
Photo credit: Carrie Vonderhaar, Ocean Futures Society.

A proportion of Cordell Bank is made up of granite reef, but much of the bank is a mixture of rock reef, boulders, cobbles, sand and mud. The diversity of the bank and its variety of habitats are important contributors to the diversity of fishes and invertebrates found on this living reef.

Sponges, hydrocorals, tunicates, anemones, gorgonians, solitary corals and hydroids compete for space on the upper-reef areas. More mobile animals like decorator crabs, sea stars, sea cucumbers, snails and demersal fishes move over the invertebrate carpet. Cover on the upper reef areas exceeds 100 percent, as animals are layered one on top of the other.

This living reef also provides critical habitat for first-year juvenile rockfishes that settle out of the water column as they transition from a pelagic to benthic life stage. Adult rockfishes, lingcod and other benthic fishes also inhabit the complex habitats within the structure of Cordell Bank. The most conspicuous invertebrates occurring in the deeper reef areas include octopus, crinoids, white plumed anemones, sea stars and tube polychaetes.

Octopus. Photo credit: Jodi Pirtle, Cordell Bank National Marine Sanctuary.

Key species within the Sanctuary

MARINE MAMMALS

Cordell Bank National Marine Sanctuary has diverse and abundant marine mammal species including 23 species of cetaceans (whales, dolphins and porpoises) and five species of pinnipeds (seals and sea lions).

Humpback whale tail. Photo credit: Robert Schwemmer, NOAA National Marine Sanctuaries.

Pacific white-sided dolphins are the most frequently sighted marine mammal in the sanctuary. Other common cetaceans observed include Dall's porpoises and northern right-whale dolphins. Endangered humpback and blue whales are regularly seen in the summer and fall when they visit the sanctuary to feed.

California sea lions are one of the most abundant pinnipeds in the sanctuary from the summer through early spring, when they are not in their breeding grounds in the south on the Channel Islands and Año Nuevo (south of San Francisco). Other mammals seen around Cordell Bank include Risso's dolphins, northern fur seals, northern elephant seals, Steller sea lions, beaked whales, harbor porpoises, minke whales and killer whales.

Risso's dolphins routinely cruise above steep drop offs of the ocean bottom in search of squid and fish. Photo credit: Carrie Vonderhaar, Ocean Futures Society.

Baleen whales, such as humpback and blue whales, feed mainly on krill and small schooling fishes, which are abundant within Cordell Bank's upwelling-driven ecosystem. In contrast, toothed whales and pinnipeds feed mainly on fishes and squid found in the sanctuary.

BLACK-FOOTED ALBATROSS

Cordell Bank's food-rich waters make it a major feeding destination for thousands of local and highly-migratory seabirds. Permanent resident bird species nest on the nearby Farallon Islands and in the Point Reyes area and feed in Cordell Bank waters. Over fifty seabird species have been identified feeding in or near the sanctuary.

Common murre in flight. Photo credit: Jennifer Stock, Cordell Bank National Marine Sanctuary.

The black-footed albatross is a large seabird with a stout body, a large head, and a somewhat elongated neck. They have exceptionally long and narrow wings, which gives them their characteristic gliding flight. They are almost completely dark in color except for white areas around some individual's bills and undertails. The black-footed albatross rarely approaches land, unless for breeding. They do not dive but pick up squid and fish at the surface when they are sitting down on the water. In the past, albatross were hunted for their feathers. Sailors used to make pipes out of their hollow bones and tobacco pouches from the webbing of their feet.

Black-footed albatross running on water. Photo credit: Steve Howell, Cordell Bank National Marine Sanctuary.

Jean-Michel was captivated by the appearance of an acquaintance from the North-western Hawaiian Islands, the wide-winged splendid black-footed albatross. Cordell Bank, we learned from sanctuary staff, is the "albatross capital of the northern hemisphere."

Dozens of species of seabirds, including tufted puffins, Cassin's auklets and sooty shearwaters, like the highly endangered black-footed albatross, have lifecycles that are inextricably linked to the California Current as a seasonal source of food. In fact, chick-rearing Hawaiian albatrosses commute across the Pacific Ocean to Cordell Bank (nearly 5,600 miles or 8960 km roundtrip) to feed on squid and fish and then deliver rich fish-oil concentrate as regurgitated meals to their fledgling chicks. Recently, scientists working with volunteers have discovered with some surprise that the black-footed albatross can make not only one but as many as three trans-Pacific Ocean flights during a single nesting season.

Black-footed albatross resting. Photo credit: Carrie Vonderhaar, Ocean Futures Society.

Black-footed albatrosses breed thousands of miles from Cordell Bank, yet still rely on the sanctuary's rich food resources to feed their young. This amazing feat was documented in a study using satellite tags; it showed that albatrosses nesting on Tern Island in the north-western Hawaiian Islands "commute" to Cordell Bank to gather food for their chicks.

FISHES

The habitats in Cordell Bank National Marine Sanctuary support more than 180 species of fishes. The most abundant are the rockfishes, ranging in size from the 8-inch (20 cm) pygmy rockfish to the 3-foot (90 cm) yellow-eye rockfish. Fish distribution and abundance on the bank are related to habitat type, depth and location.

Copper rockfish. Photo credit: Carrie Vonderhaar, Ocean Futures Society.

- ***Rocky Bank Fishes***

  The shallow, rocky pinnacle regions of the central bank are dominated by schooling species such as yellowtail, blue and widow rockfish along with first year juvenile rockfishes. Boulder-rock habitats are home to rockfishes, lingcod, painted greenling and the blackeyed goby. Boulder habitats at the edge of the bank host large communities of commercially-important species, such as bocaccio, yelloweye and canary rockfishes as well as lingcod. Cordell Bank is an important site for the success of juvenile rockfishes transitioning to their adult life stage. These first-year juveniles are important prey for salmon, seabirds and adult rockfishes as they provide an important energetic link in the food chain of this system.

Bocaccio rockfish. Photo credit: Dave Murfin, NOAA.

- ***Soft Bottom Fishes***

  The soft bottom habitat in the sanctuary, which ranges from 240 to 1,640 feet (73 to 500 meters) in depth, is an ideal home for flatfishes, skates, and rays. In addition, a number of spindle-shaped fishes such as rockfishes and sculpins also thrive there.

Longnose skate. Photo credit: Dave Murfin, NOAA.

- ***Pelagic (open-ocean) Fishes***

  Most of the water column habitat within the sanctuary overlies the continental shelf and makes up the coastal pelagic realm. While few directed studies have been performed at this sanctuary, a considerable amount is known about California's coastal pelagic fishes.

  Fishes that occupy the shallow epipelagic zone (depth to 164 feet/50 meters) are relatively large, active, fast-growing and long-lived. Fishes commonly placed in this group include sharks (blue, white and thresher), jack mackerel, Pacific mackerel, Pacific hake, and Albacore Tuna. The ocean sunfish is among the most common pelagic fishes in the sanctuary. We also know that the early life-history stages of many fishes—such as lingcod, rockfishes and many flatfish species—occupy the epipelagic zone. Anadramous fishes, including coho and chinook salmon and steelhead, seasonally occur in the sanctuary.

  Mesopelagic fishes (those found below the epipelagic zone, to depths of 3,280 feet/1,000 meters) are relatively small, slow-growing and long-lived. Representatives of this group include the lanternfishes, hatchetfishes and deep-sea smelts.

Pelagic species, like this blue shark, have wide ranging distributions and can be found in all the west coast sanctuaries. Photo credit: Matthew Ferraro, Ocean Futures Society.

INVERTEBRATES

- ### *Benthic (seafloor) Invertebrates*

  A dense cover of benthic invertebrates carpets the shallower rock surfaces of Cordell Bank. The abundant food supply of plankton drifting over the bank, combined with a hard surface for larvae to settle out and attach provide ideal conditions where space is a limiting factor. Invertebrate cover on the upper reef areas can exceed 100 percent as sponges, corals, sea squirts, anemones, and hydroids compete for space. More mobile invertebrate animals like decorator crabs, sea stars, sea cucumbers and snails move over and around this dense invertebrate carpet.

  The soft bottom habitats within the sanctuary also support a thriving community of benthic invertebrates. Adapted to life in and on a shifting habitat, these animals are either buried in the sediment, like polychaete worms and clams, or move around on the surface, such as sea stars and Dungeness crabs.

Polychaete worm extending tentacles. Photo credit: Cordell Bank Expeditions.

Sea stars and orange cup coral. Photo credit: Michael Carver, Cordell Bank National Marine Sanctuary.

The sea whip is one common soft bottom resident that extends into the water column providing structure and habitat for fishes and other invertebrates on the flat, mostly featureless bottom of the continental shelf.

- *Humboldt squid*

  Humboldt squid have been migrating farther north up the California coast and even as far north as Alaska for reasons that aren't completely understood by scientists. What we do know about Humboldt squid is that it's a deepwater species and, like most cephalopods, has a short lifespan. Humboldt squid reach an impressive six feet (1.8 meters) plus in a lifespan of only one to two years. To reach that length in such a relatively short time, they have to be voracious. But why are they moving north? Is it global change and warming water temperatures? Are they finding new niches that have now been opened because larger pelagic fish populations are in decline? Or are they following their favorite prey?

  In doing some of the research for America's Underwater Treasures, we had read that within the vicinity of Cordell Bank National Marine Sanctuary there was fishing for Humboldt squid on a daily basis. One report that really stood out in my mind was that at the end of February 2006, in one day, one sport-fishing boat landed over 700 squid. It really sparked Jean-Michel's interest to try to better understand why they're found so far north in such large concentrations. Is this now an annual migration? Are they coming up from the south or are they coming up from deeper water? So we met with a fishing captain and he explained the whole fishing process. It's really easy to attract the squid using a large gig with a bright neon color to mimic one of their favorite prey items, the lantern fish.

  These squid are cannibals so once they see one of their teammates [LAUGHS] injured or stressed or struggling, it's an opportunity to feed. So with a few on the gig, you get the whole group coming up to shallow depths and it's easy to

Two Humboldt squid size each other up. Photo credit: Carrie Vonderhaar, Ocean Futures Society.

catch them quickly. Our question was about the sustainability of it. Is this now going to be an annual event off northern California? It was a chance to ask questions about sustainable fisheries management. The challenge, though, is that we need first to understand the life cycle and distribution patterns of Humboldt squid if it's to be a well-managed fishery.

So in anticipation of the opportunity to film them at Cordell Banks, we got a cage, not to protect the team from sharks but from the squid, an animal that not many people would believe is dangerous, but the Humboldt squid can be. — Holly Lohuis, Education/Research Associate, Ocean Futures Society.

The Humboldt squid may reach six feet long and live from one to four years.
Photo credit: Carrie Vonderhaar, Ocean Futures Society.

Our biggest concern was that these squid basically will eat anything and they're known to wrap themselves around divers and then pull them down very quickly. Divers have burst eardrums and there's the potential to get really harmed. People who have filmed them or dive with them on a regular basis wear a lot of body armor, mesh suits, hockey armor; they're very well protected, head to toe.—Carrie Vonderhaar, Chief Expedition Photographer, Ocean Futures Society.

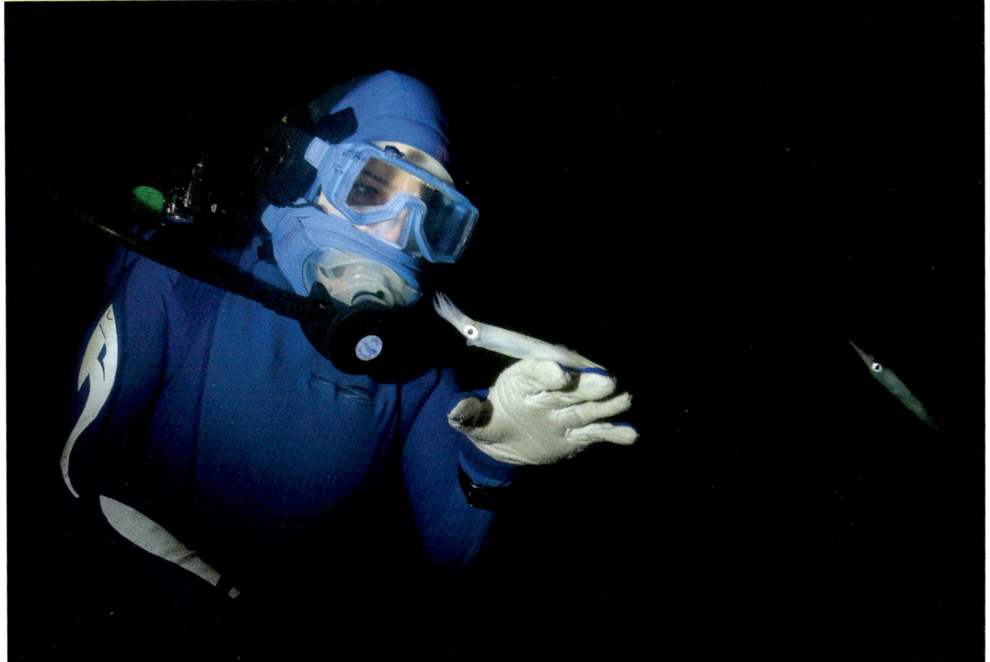

Market squid are only several inches long. Photo credit: Carrie Vonderhaar, Ocean Futures Society.

Humboldt squid have appeared in record numbers at Cordell Bank National Marine Sanctuary leading to speculation that they may be expanding their range northward. Ocean Futures Society's marine biologist Holly Lohuis is tethered by steel cable to the surface ship because Humboldt squid are capable of dragging divers to deep water. Photo credit: Carrie Vonderhaar, Ocean Futures Society.

Two of them, a little one and the largest one in the group, broke away and swam right up to the surface, just below the boat. Then all of a sudden the little one disappeared. By little I mean about two feet (60 cm) long compared to the other at about four-and-a-half feet (140 cm). But I didn't really put two and two together until we were back up on the surface and our guide told us that the big one ate the little one. There were no floating body parts; the smaller one was just gone. These animals don't waste anything. When they eat, they eat the whole thing. Their beaks are sharp like a parrot's beak and they'll take chunks out of a body in a bite. When you see the tentacles spread apart and the beak comes out at you...it's very impressive.—Holly Lohuis, Education/ Research Associate, Ocean Futures Society.

Ocean Futures Society's marine biologist, Holly Lohuis reveals the Humboldt squid's impressive mouth with a razor-sharp beak ringed by barbed suckers that cling to prey. Photo credit: Carrie Vonderhaar, Ocean Futures Society.

- ***Krill***

  Small, shrimp-like crustaceans, known as krill, serve an important role in the sanctuary's food chain. Krill are referred to as "keystone" species because they are critical prey for so many other species on and around the bank. During the spring and summer, massive swarms of krill provide food for dominant species of the Cordell Bank ecosystem including seabirds, fishes and whales.

Céline Cousteau swims through a blizzard of plankton and krill.
Photo credit: Carrie Vonderhaar, Ocean Futures Society.

Research within the Sanctuary

Research projects in the sanctuary include the following:

- **Cordell Bank Species List:** The goal of the Cordell Bank Species List is to create a comprehensive database of all species documented within the Cordell Bank National Marine Sanctuary. The species list is actively being updated to include new observations of birds, marine mammals, fishes, invertebrates and algae observed in the sanctuary. For the first time in thirty years, a dive team explored the reef crest at Cordell Bank in October 2010. They collected specimens, photographs and video footage for analysis.

- **Cordell Bank Condition Report:** The Cordell Bank National Marine Sanctuary Condition Report provides a summary of resources in the sanctuary, pressures on those resources, the current condition and trends, and management responses to the pressures that threaten the integrity of the marine environment. Specifically, the report includes information on the status and trends of water quality, habitat, living resources and maritime archaeological resources and the human activities that affect them.

- **Deep Sea Coral Habitat Modeling:** Deep Sea Coral Habitats are being studied using a combination of observation data from the *Delta* submersible, remotely-operated vehicles and autonomous underwater vehicles, and sampling data collected by multibeam acoustic samplers.

- **Integrated Ecological Studies:** These projects study the spatial and temporal relationships between oceanographic processes, zooplankton, and marine birds and mammals in the region surrounding Cordell Bank and the Gulf of the Farallones.

Diver assessing condition of reef. Photo credit: Cordell Bank Expeditions.

Research Assets

R/V *FULMAR*

The National Marine Sanctuary Program's 67-foot (20-meter) R/V *Fulmar* is used for research, education and emergency response programs for the West Coast region. The vessel is homeported at the Monterey Harbor in the Monterey Bay National Marine Sanctuary, and also serves the Gulf of the Farallones and Cordell Bank National Marine Sanctuaries. When the vessel works at Cordell Bank, it is ported at Spud Point Marina in Bodega Bay.

Research vessel Fulmar. Photo credit: NOAA National Marine Sanctuaries.

NOAA SHIP *MCARTHUR II*

The NOAA ship *McArthur II* conducts oceanographic research and assessments through-out the eastern Pacific, including the U.S. West Coast, plus Central and South America. The *McArthur II* is involved in studies in several of the national marine sanctuaries on the west coast of the United States. The 224-foot (68-meter) ship engages in measurements of chemical, meteorological, and biological sampling for several large scale programs within NOAA. Cordell Bank National Marine Sanctuary often uses the *McArthur II* to conduct operations that are more feasible from a larger vessel.

R/V McArthur II. Photo credit: Chad King, Monterey Bay National Marine Sanctuary.

HUMAN OCCUPIED VEHICLE (HOV)

An HOV is a vessel capable of carrying one or more observers beneath the sea in a pressurized environment. Cordell Bank National Marine Sanctuary has utilized the *Delta* submersible, which accommodates a pilot and scientist and reaches depths to 1,100 feet (335 m). The *Delta* is equipped with video and audio recorders, which allow scientists to record their observations. HOVs are expensive and challenging to operate when compared with remotely-operated vehicles (ROVs), but they allow the scientist to directly experience the ocean environment with resolution superior to that provided by remote video systems. The safety requirements of occupied submersible operations add to the cost and complexity of HOV operations. An HOV is recommended in high relief habitats and/or when detailed observations by a human observer are required.

Submersible "Delta" after surfacing. Photo credit: Chad King, Monterey Bay National Marine Sanctuary.

REMOTELY-OPERATED VEHICLE (ROV)

Remotely-operated vehicles (ROVs) are tethered undersea robots that are usually operated from vessels to perform a variety of observational and collecting tasks. An ROV typically consists of a frame onto which equipment matched to the task at hand is mounted. Most ROVs have thrusters that provide mobility, cameras and lighting systems for visibility, and manipulator arms for collecting samples. Cordell Bank National Marine Sanctuary co-owns (with Monterey Bay and Gulf of the Farallones National Marine Sanctuaries) a relatively small work class ROV (Phantom HD2) which has a working depth capability of about 1000 feet (300m). The ROV is equipped with an optical zoom high-resolution video color camera with 90 degree tilt, high power lights, a three-finger manipulator arm, and paired lasers for sizing objects in the video camera's field of view. The Phantom ROV is smaller, less expensive to operate and capable of longer dives than an HOV. The ROV is recommended for use in habitats of moderate complexity where entanglement of the umbilical cable is a low probability and video imagery alone is suitable to characterize the habitat and biological community. ROVs cannot be used when high winds or currents complicate coordination of the ROV with the surface support vessel.

ROV being deployed. Photo credit: Cordell Bank National Marine Sanctuary.

TOWED CAMERA SLED

The Cordell Bank National Marine Sanctuary towed camera sled is similar in basic design to the ROV except that it is not equipped with thrusters. Instead, the sled is towed through the water by a surface vessel. Similar to the Phantom ROV, the camera sled also has high power lights, an optical zoom video color camera, and paired lasers for sizing objects in the video camera's field of view. The sled is co-owned by Cordell Bank, Monterey Bay and Gulf of the Farallones National Marine Sanctuaries. Since it has no thrusters, the sled is much simpler to maintain and operate than the ROV. The sled is considerably less maneuverable than an ROV, and therefore, its use is generally restricted to low relief habitats to minimize encounters with collision and entanglement hazards. The sled performs better in high wind and current conditions than the ROV.

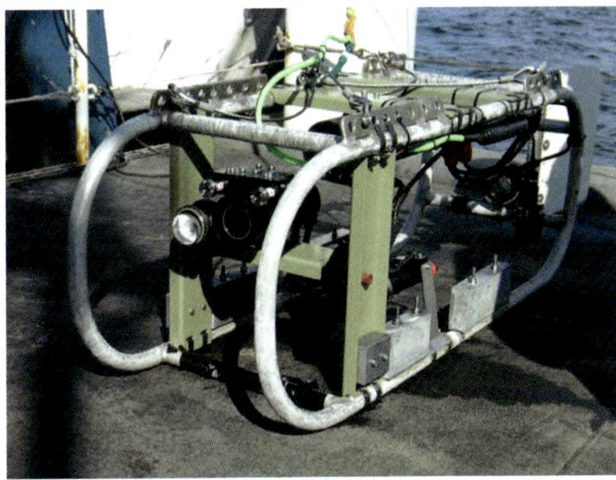

Camera sled provided by the Cordell Bank National Marine Sanctuary to document seafloor habitat and species. Photo credit: NOAA National Marine Sanctuaries.

Visiting the Sanctuary

Note: In the last section of the book, "When You Visit the Sanctuaries," is detailed information about resources found within each sanctuary to help visitors have an enjoyable and productive visit.

VISITOR'S CENTER

Cordell Bank National Marine Sanctuary does not have its own visitor's center. However, if you are traveling along the California coast, you can learn more about Cordell Bank at the Point Reyes National Seashore Visitor Center, Gulf of the Farallones National Marine Sanctuary Visitor Center at Crissy Field (see page 187) or Bodega Marine Laboratory in Bodega Bay.

Visitors learn about Cordell Bank at Point Reyes National Seashore Visitor Center. Photo credit: NOAA National Marine Sanctuaries.

Sanctuary administrative office location

The Cordell Bank National Marine Sanctuary office is located at the administration area at Point Reyes National Seashore, just across the way from the Seashore Headquarters in the giant red barn.

Cordell Bank National Marine Sanctuary office

1 Bear Valley Rd.
Point Reyes Station, CA 94956

Mailing address:

PO Box 159
Olema, CA 94950
Telephone: 415-663-0314

From June until November, humpback and blue whales may be seen eagerly feeding in the sanctuary. Throughout the year, seabirds from near and far feed in these bountiful waters. This attracts birders and whale watchers from around the world to see species rarely seen so close to shore.

Watching humpback whales. Photo credit: Gary E. Davis.

Exploring the Cordell Bank National Marine Sanctuary can take many forms. Whether on a boat "wildlife watching," visiting the University of California Davis' Bodega Marine Laboratory, or at the Aquarium of the Bay, one can learn about the underwater species found throughout Cordell Bank. Other opportunities in the area allow for fishing, crabbing, sailing and boating. While commercial trips to Cordell Bank National Marine Sanctuary are not offered regularly, guided naturalist tours often leave from Bodega Harbor allowing visitors to get an up close view of the sanctuary and learn about the extreme biological productivity that takes place in the waters of Cordell Bank. Pelagic birding trips to Cordell Bank are offered about six times a year.

ECO-TOURISM

Yearly, Cordell Bank National Marine Sanctuary co-sponsors a field seminar with Point Reyes National Seashore Association's Field Seminar Program to introduce participants to the offshore wildlife that makes Cordell Bank so special. Scholarships are available to make this fee-based program available to teachers at no charge. Check the events calendar[1] for dates and more information. The Field Seminar Program comprises a half-day classroom seminar followed by a full day boat trip to the sanctuary. The seminar provides an introduction to Cordell Bank's seafloor habitats, the pelagic seabirds that might be seen during the boat trip, and an explanation about why and how marine mammals and seabirds come from so far away to feed in this region. The seminar also allows participants to get acquainted before getting on a moving vessel.

Sunrise over the Sonoma coast. Photo credit; Michael Carver, Cordell Bank National Marine Sanctuary.

---

1   http://cordellbank.noaa.gov/news/calendar.html

The field portion of the Field Seminar Program is led by naturalists/marine biologists who are experienced on the water. During the cruise out to the bank region, participants may see pods of Pacific white-sided dolphins, Dall's porpoise, blue and humpback whales, California and Steller sea lions, elephant seals and numerous seabirds such as shearwaters, albatross, skuas, jaegers, rhinocerous auklets and/or puffins and more. This full-day boat trip travels almost 100 miles (160 km) in nine hours.

BOATING

Because the sanctuary is entirely offshore, it can only be visited by boat, and even then, only in good weather. September and October are the best months, when calm seas and light winds make the trip smoother and the marine life easier to see. In order to protect the fragile reef community, anchoring is prohibited in areas shallower than 300 feet (91 meters). The sanctuary office can issue special permits for research or education purposes.

DIVING

Recreational diving is not recommended at Cordell Bank for a number of reasons. The upper reef areas on Cordell Bank are between 115 and 140 feet (35 and 43 meters) and Cordell Bank typically has strong currents that are extremely variable and can run in opposite directions at different depths.

Sea conditions 20 miles (32 km) from shore can change rapidly, even on days that start calmly. Fog and wind can develop quickly, making dive conditions treacherous. Visibility is variable from good to green and ocean temperatures usually hover around 50°F (10°C).

(L-R) Ocean Futures Society's Chief Expedition Photographer Carrie Vonderhaar and Fabien Cousteau ready to dive Cordell Bank on close-circuit rebreathers. Photo credit: Holly Lohuis, Ocean Futures Society.

The team knew that the dives at Cordell Bank would be challenging. The fact is that even though it is a National Marine Sanctuary because of its amazing abundance of marine life, especially animal life, it is the least accessible sanctuary even to divers and scientists. Its glory is far below the surface, and few divers have ventured to Cordell Bank in over ten years because of the wild seas that guard it.

Even though we went on a "favorable" day (LAUGHS), the fact is that we started with eight-foot swells and it went beyond that by the end of the dive. The currents were extremely strong, and we were diving to depths beyond the sport-diving limit, so it was extremely challenging and physically exerting. But all that made the payoff of actually getting down there even sweeter. —Fabien Cousteau

In heaving seas and a ripping current, Ocean Futures Society team members Jacob Kilbride and Zim Gervais work to pull Fabien Cousteau onto the stern of the vessel Superfish. Photo credit: Chuck Davis, Ocean Futures Society (High Definition Video Frame Grab).

FISHING

For more than a century, Cordell Bank has been a destination fishing ground for both sport and commercial fishing. Due to intensive fishing of deep-water species (particularly groundfishes) in the 1980's, many populations were depleted. Consequently, some species have been declared overfished by the Pacific Fishery Management Council, and fishing activity within the sanctuary is now limited to allow these fish stocks to recover. A large portion of the sanctuary has been designated as either rockfish conservation or essential fish habitat closure area.[2] Groundfishing is not allowed within these areas. Outside of these areas, recreational fishing at Cordell Bank is managed by the California Department of Fish and Game[3] and the National Marine Fisheries Service.[4]

Greenspotted rockfish. Photo credit: Dave Murfin, NOAA.

---

2   http://santuaries.noaa.gov/science/condition/cbnms/images/fig23_lg.jpg

3   http://www.dfg.ca.gov/marine/

4   http://www.nwr.noaa.gov/Groundfish-Halibut/Groundfish-Fishery-Management/Ground-fish-Closed-Areas/Index.cfm#CP_JUMP_30284

Olympic Coast National Marine Sanctuary

About Olympic Coast National Marine Sanctuary

Aerial view of the Olympic Coast. Photo credit: Olympic Coast National Marine Sanctuary.

Designated in July 1994, Olympic Coast National Marine Sanctuary spans 135 miles (216 km) of coastline, including the northwestern-most point in the lower 48 United States, Cape Flattery. It shares 64 miles (103 km) of coastline with Olympic National Park. Encompassing an area of 3,310 square miles (8,570 km²), the sanctuary is nearly two-and-a-half times the size of Olympic National Park. Its sparsely-populated shoreline includes more than 52 miles (84 km) of wilderness beaches. The sanctuary extends 25 to 50 miles (40–80 km) seaward, covering much of the continental shelf and several major submarine canyons. It protects a productive upwelling zone—home to rich marine mammal and seabird faunas, diverse populations of kelp and intertidal algae, and thriving invertebrate communities.

Visitors can explore miles of sand and cobble beaches and dramatic, rocky shoreline with tide pools, offshore islands and sea stacks. Birders will find large colonies of seabirds such as murres and tufted puffins, as well as one of the largest populations of bald eagles in the lower 48 states. During annual migrations, more than a million seabirds, waterfowl and shorebirds travel along this coast.

Twenty-nine species of marine mammals are found here. These waters also teem with fishes. Seven species of salmon, along with halibut, rockfish, herring, sturgeon and others support important sport, tribal and commercial fisheries.

These waters are also rich in human history. Native peoples—the Hoh, Makah, Quileute and Quinault—have lived along this coast for thousands of years, as they continue to do today. Heavily-used historical and contemporary trade routes run through Olympic Coast National Marine Sanctuary. More than 180 ships lie wrecked on the seafloor along this rugged and stormy coast, but only a handful have been verified, mapped and assessed.[1]

Clownlike in appearance, tufted puffins nest on a few islands within the sanctuary. Their numbers have dwindled over the decades, for unknown reasons. Photo credit: Olympic Coast National Marine Sanctuary.

This anchor is nearly all that remains of the bark Austria, grounded at Cape Alava in 1887. Photo credit: Olympic Coast National Marine Sanctuary.

---

1   http://channelislands.noaa.gov/shipwreck/dbase.html

Why a National Marine Sanctuary?

Lying adjacent to expansive stretches of spectacular undeveloped shoreline, Olympic Coast National Marine Sanctuary represents one of North America's most productive marine ecosystems. The sanctuary encompasses a variety of habitat types, from sand beaches and rocky intertidal shores to nearshore kelp forests and uninhabited islands, to deep coral and sponge communities and submarine canyons. The sanctuary's temperate location and complex physical environment maintain critical habitats for unique communities of organisms.

Shoreline of the Olympic Coast National Marine Sanctuary shrouded in fog.
Photo credit: Carrie Vonderhaar, Ocean Futures Society.

A long history of human interaction with the marine environment is a unique facet of the area's legacy. Native American cultures have lived for millennia in an intimate relationship with the ocean. Beginning in the 16th century, European exploration and settlement made a significant impact on the Olympic Coast. Beyond severe natural forces, the principal threats to maritime archaeological resources in the sanctuary come from unauthorized salvage and contact by fishing gear.

Dwindling salmon runs and shortened seasons have adversely affected Olympic Coast's once thriving commercial charter fishing industry. Photo credit: Olympic Coast National Marine Sanctuary.

Of the 29 species of marine mammals found in the sanctuary, 12 are considered threatened, endangered, or species of concern at the state or federal level. Some animals, like the California gray whale, have made significant recovery since protections were put into place. The original Washington population of sea otters was completely hunted out by the early 1900's but is now making a comeback, thanks to a tenacious reintroduction program that began in the late 1970's. Unfortunately, other species' declines, such as the southern population of resident Orca, have only recently come to light.

Southern sea otter. Otters will keep their rear feet out of the water like this to warm up (thermo-regulate). Photo credit: Josh Pederson, SIMoN/NOAA.

The Mission Statement:

"To protect the Olympic Coast's natural and cultural resources through responsible stewardship, to conduct and apply research to preserve the area's ecological integrity and maritime heritage, and to promote understanding through public outreach and education."

Resources within Olympic Coast National Marine Sanctuary

TIDE POOLS

The Washington coast and Strait of Juan de Fuca have two high and low tides each day. A highest high and a lowest low tide are followed by a moderate high tide and a moderate low tide. Tidal changes along the coast are large, averaging about 12 feet (3.5 meters). Tide pools occur where boulders and rocky outcrops trap seawater when the tide recedes. At high tide, they form surge channels, crevices and cracks that are home to many familiar seashore animals, like sea stars, hermit crabs and sea anemones. Scientists have identified over 300 resident species of aquatic plants, invertebrates (animals without backbones) and fish here. This number may be but a fraction of the species that actually inhabit this stretch of coast.

Most intertidal plants and animals have elaborate life cycles that usually include a free-floating, planktonic phase. At some point in this cycle, they settle down, adhering to the rock or burrowing into the sand within the intertidal zone. Some intertidal inhabitants are surprisingly long-lived: the rock scallop, for instance, can live for more than a century.

Some intertidal animals actively hunt and capture prey. Among the most impressive of these is the ochre sea star—a bright purple or orange creature that moves slowly into shallow water to feed on California mussels and other stationary invertebrates at high tide.

Exploring the rocky intertidal in the Olympic Coast National Marine Sanctuary. Photo credit: Claire Fackler, NOAA National Marine Sanctuaries.

Every surface in the rocky intertidal zone is used by something. Predatory ochre sea stars roam among communities of green sea anemones and rockweed searching for mussels. Photo credit: Nancy Sefton, NOAA.

Others draw strength from their neighbors. This is especially evident within beds of mussels, whose numerous nooks and crannies are known to provide shelter for over 200 species of small organisms. A similar function is served by the various red algae that grow in dense mats, under which many animals hide from predators, wave action or stressful conditions at low tide.

Many species have entered into curious partnerships with other life forms. The giant green anemone is one of these: its bright hues are the product of microscopic green algae, which grow in the anemone's digestive tract. Scientists think that the compounds produced by the algae may help feed the anemone.

Green Anemone. Photo credit: Brian Hall, Ocean Futures Society.

Because they contain so many interesting life forms, tide pools are often damaged by care-less trampling and collecting. Visitors should take care in order to experience and enjoy these special habitats without damaging them. Bare rock is less slippery than rocks covered with algae; by stepping on bare rock, people will also avoid stepping on the animals and plants that cling to these surfaces. After looking underneath rocks in the intertidal zone, people should replace them in their original positions to protect those plants and animals that live on or under them. Visitors should never force an animal off its spot—rough or excessive handling may hurt it.

FIRST PEOPLE

All along the Pacific Coast, native people have drawn from the ocean's bounty. They have made their living as hunters, gatherers and fishers, made jewelry and ornaments from shells, and traded up and down the coast. They lived here for many thousands of years before the arrival of Europeans to the Pacific Coast. The newcomers exploited native tribes for labor and resources, introduced diseases that decimated entire tribes and sought to stamp out ages-old cultural traditions. But native peoples, though fewer in number, still survive up and down the Pacific Coast. Many still carry on native traditions, and some tribes still stand as sovereign nations in their ancestral lands.

California mussels and barnacles. Photo credit: Olympic Coast National Marine Sanctuary.

Tribal dancers. Photo credit: Olympic Coast National Marine Sanctuary.

Their ancestors lived along the Olympic Coast for at least 6,000 years. The sea was central to their cultures from the food they ate to the art they produced. These people were intimately attuned to the tides, currents and seasons. They hunted seals and whales, gathered crabs and mussels, fished for halibut, salmon and lingcod and gathered kelp to eat and to use for medicine.

Four tribes—the Makah, Hoh, Quileute and Quinalt—still live on the Olympic Coast as sovereign nations. Today, they hold to their traditional culture while serving as managers of the natural resources on their lands. The sanctuary supports them in their cultural revival and helps protect their cultural legacy. Olympic Coast sanctuary staff supported a canoe journey made by all tribes along the length of the coast, allowing a new generation of the ocean-going peoples to experience the traditions of their ancestors. Working with others under the supervision of the Makah, the sanctuary is involved in archeological studies of village and midden or refuse sites on their land.

Human presence on the Olympic Coast predates historical record and attests to the subtle understandings of the marine environment. Photo credit: Olympic Coast National Marine Sanctuary.

Native American canoes in Port Angeles, Washington, in celebration of the 2004 CoastFest events. Photo credit: Claire Fackler, NOAA National Marine Sanctuaries.

The tribes play crucial roles in assisting the sanctuary to shape policy, research and education programs through ongoing consultations, joint projects, and as members of the Sanctuary Advisory Council. On a day-to-day basis the sanctuary and the tribes act collaboratively, different perspectives focusing on the long-term health of a common priceless ecological and cultural legacy.

Key species within the Sanctuary

FISHES

Cold, temperate waters of the Olympic Coast are some of the most productive fish-growing habitats in the world. Long known for salmon and halibut, the Olympic Coast is also rich in rockfish and other ecologically-important fish species. Historically, many commercial fisheries were developed on the Olympic Coast, including harvests of halibut, hake and salmon. Before that, Native Americans fished the plentiful waters using a wide variety of net and line techniques. Most important, however, is the sheer abundance and diversity of fish species that are not used by people, but which form the web of living things holding the complex ecosystem together. Predator and prey alike, from vast shoals of herring to solitary ocean sunfish, fish are indicators of ocean health.

Giant ocean sunfish often reach eight feet in length. These odd-looking fish swim lazily through the water, feeding primarily on jellyfish. Photo credit: Steve Fisher, NOAA.

Salmon are anadromous fish, meaning that they spend most of their life in salt water but return to fresh water to spawn at maturity. Five species of Pacific salmon occur along the outer coast of Washington: chinook, sockeye, pink, chum, and coho. Two other salmon-related anadromous species, sea-run cutthroat trout and steelhead, also inhabit offshore waters. Four of the top ten fishes commercially harvested along the outer coast of Washington (chinook, coho, and chum salmon, and lingcod) are either estuarine-associated (i.e., they use estuaries during some time in their lives) or estuarine-dependent (i.e., they require estuaries to complete their life cycles). Additionally, the top four recreational species for Washington (chinook and coho salmon, steelhead, and lingcod) all utilize estuaries, at least as juveniles.

Sockeye salmon. Photo credit: NOAA.

WOLF EELS

When fully mature, wolf eels may reach seven feet (2.1 meters) long and weigh up to 40 pounds (18 kg). They swim by flexing 350 vertebrae (compared with the 34 vertebrae of humans) to move their long sinuous forms from head to tail. Young wolf eels are the color of bright copper but turn more gray and mottled with age, ultimately becoming patterned with dark spots that cover the ultra-fine scales of their slippery skins. Wolf eels live in the western Pacific Ocean from Alaska to San Diego, from subtidal zones to 740 feet (226 meters).

A wolf eel coming out of its den, Olympic Coast National Marine Sanctuary.
Photo Credit: Carrie Vonderhaar, Ocean Futures Society.

Slithery, fast, big teeth—that's the startling impression divers get when this grizzled-looking face darts from beneath a rocky crevice or reef. And with bulging eyes and a bald head lending a quizzical look to this hunchback's fearsome grin, it's hard not to

Wolf eels eat sea urchins, spines and all. Photo Credit: Carrie Vonderhaar, Ocean Futures Society.

wonder if they are more an accident of nature than a thought out plan. But beyond bizarre looks, we know the behaviors of wolf eels are equally fascinating to observe. Watching one feed, for instance, can be an awe-inspiring sight. Their square, protruding jaws crunch whole clams and mussels, and, in a rather alarming way, bite through sea urchins, spines and all. They will also feast on soft invertebrates like sea cucumbers and octopuses, snapping their jaws shut on their prey like an alligator, then flipping, spinning, and tearing flesh as they roll. When not foraging around the kelp forest or seafloor, wolf eels retreat to their resident caves.

Wolf eels mate for life. Photo credit: Carrie Vonderhaar, Ocean Futures Society.

Wolf eels bite through clamshells and other prey with strong teeth and powerful jaws. Photo credit: Carrie Vonderhaar, Ocean Futures Society.

By the age of four, this roving predator will settle into a more sedentary lifestyle, seeking out and bonding with a mate, then sharing a single den for the rest of their lives. Wolf eel courtship is a rough and tumble affair. It begins with the male first nudging its mate in the belly before coiling around the female to fertilize the eggs as they are being laid, up to 10,000 at a time. Both parents take turns caring for the nest, alternately guarding, hunting and feeding for 13 to 16 weeks until the eggs hatch and the offspring emerge.

"To me a wolf eel looks like a very old lady. Or maybe it's a very old man (LAUGHS). Or a grandmother. It blows my mind to see these animals crush shellfish the way they do to feed. I mean it should hurt to do that. And I find it amazing that they live together like a happy old couple. They stay in the same place together, very predictable. I mean it's like looking at people. It's strange. I wish we had a team of divers to sit under water in front of one wolf eel couple and spend a week watching what they do, trying to understand. Who goes for the groceries? What else do they do? They mate for life and apparently if anything happens to one of them and there are eggs to protect, the other one will curl up around the eggs and not eat or leave until they hatch. That's amazing for a fish. Even though no one specifically tries to catch them, they do get caught and have been served as 'ocean catfish.' I like the fact that they're called wolf eels and they have nothing to do with either wolves or eels. It makes us think about our own misconceptions and fears, doesn't it? It also makes us think to realize they have such a close and enduring relationship. Obviously, they love each other, or the equivalent of that to a fish."—Jean-Michel Cousteau

GIANT PACIFIC OCTOPUS

Octopuses are wily creatures with many tricks, like specialized cells containing cap-sules of pigment that when squeezed or expanded produce hundreds of hues. And with a lightning twitch of muscles, they can morph forms, changing textures that vary from horny or warty to completely smooth. It is camouflage of the most accomplished degree, evolution's sleight of hand, that has helped this cunning, soft-bodied carni-vore shed the hard shell of its mollusc kin—the spiral-shelled gastropods, conch and tritons, and hinged bivalved cousins, scallops and clams.

Ocean Futures Society's Director of Photography, Matt Ferraro comes face-to-face with a giant of the deep. Photo credit: Carrie Vonderhaar, Ocean Futures Society.

Related to squid, cuttlefish, and nautilus, the giant Pacific octopus is among the largest of its family in the sea. And they may reach up to 600 pounds (272 kg) with an arm span of 25 feet (7.6 meters), but along the Olympic Coast and Puget Sound, where we first encountered them, they are more commonly a quarter of this size. Giant octopuses live in the intertidal zone to depths of 1,650 feet (500 meters) at the edge of the deep abyssal plain, from southern California to Alaska and across the Aleutian Islands to Japan. They lead mostly solitary lives and avoid their own kind, except for one act of mating before death. Males find females by following a trail of pheromones, chemical cues they release into the sea. No long drawn–out courtship here. Pairing is short-lived and after mating, they will each go their separate ways.

On her own, the female octopus hunts for a suitable site to brood her offspring, then entombs herself with stones and sand. Gluing the eggs in strings to the roof of her lair, the mother will slowly, carefully deposit tens of thousands of tiny seed-like pearls. She guards them for up to seven months, in the coldest water temperatures, less time in warmer regions, aerating the embryos with jets of water and gently cleaning away algae and debris. When the larvae emerge, they swim to the surface to join other plankton drifters until weeks later, when they'll settle to the seafloor.

Octopuses take advantage of jet propulsion to move quickly. Photo credit: Carrie Vonderhaar, Ocean Futures Society.

Neither parent lives beyond the birth of their offspring. Females who've fasted while brooding their eggs will crawl from their lairs to die, becoming a meal for crabs, sea stars and other roving scavengers of the sea. After mating, large old males sometimes go senile as they near the end of their days. The few young that survive to adulthood will outgrow all but a handful of larger predators in three to four years. Only the lingcod, halibut, and the roving wolves of the sea—seals and sea lions—will hunt for them. And if cornered, these illusionists have a means of last escape—a blast of purple ink, a smoke screen diversion and jet-like propulsion to spirit them away. While their soft bodies may be vulnerable to the teeth of large carnivores, eight formidable arms reaching 25 feet (7.6 meters) create a powerful vise from which few of their captured prey ever escape. It's been estimated, in fact, that upwards of forty pounds (18 kg) of pull is needed to release the grip of a mere three-pound (1.4 kg) octopus.

The tentacles of a giant octopus are lined with suckers that grasp prey.
Photo credit: Carrie Vonderhaar, Ocean Futures Society.

Rows of giant suckers, 280 per tentacle, are arrayed with chemoreceptors, a type of sensory organ giant Pacific octopuses use to investigate their surroundings simultaneously through touch and smell. For a stealthy nighttime marauder, these sophisticated senses are useful for prowling around in the dark in search of crabs, fish and mollusks, their favorite meals. The shells of clams and scallops are wrenched open using hydraulic muscle force, but whatever refuses to yield to this octopod's grip falls under the attack of their sharp horny beaks, which are lethally effective at ripping apart prey. Octopuses have three hearts that pump blue blood, and large sensitive eyes, the closest of any invertebrates to our own. And they may share some other characteristics originally thought unique to mammals; they appear to play, demonstrate distinct personalities, and show emotions. If disturbed by divers, a giant octopus may flash colors to display its moods. Scientists suspect that white signals fear, red warns of anger and brown reflects a state of calm—transformations all the more extraordinary given that cephalopods are completely colorblind. Their clever minds are experts at solving puzzles and staging disappearing acts, much to the dismay of aquarists who've learned they are a handful to keep entertained and enclosed.

SEABIRDS

*Caspian terns.
Photo credit: Olympic
Coast National Marine
Sanctuary.*

Seabirds, ranging in size from tiny storm-petrels to majestic black-footed albatross, roam over the wave tops offshore in Olympic Coast National Marine Sanctuary. Sea stacks and islands provide critical nesting habitat for common murres and tufted puffins. Sand and gravel beaches furnish habitat for shorebirds, crows, gulls and a host of others. The coastline forms an important migratory pathway for millions of birds that pass through each year, guiding ducks, geese, cranes and raptors toward northern breeding areas during the spring and southward as winter approaches.

Imagine a bird the size of a robin surviving on the open seas. A bird like a fork-tailed storm-petrel, which weighs less than a stick of butter and is covered with seemingly fragile feathers, can weather winter storms, drink saltwater for refreshment and sleep comfortably on the rollicking waves. Pelagic (ocean-living) birds live dramatic lives and seem to get along quite well in harsh aquatic environments. They would shun land completely except for one critical period of their lives—breeding. Marine birds must return to the land in order to lay their eggs and during this time, they crowd onto the most remote, severe pieces of real estate they can find—the offshore islands and sea stacks. Some, like rhinoceros auklets, Cassin's auklets and storm-petrels burrow into any available soil and deposit an egg deep underground. Others, like common murres and the cormorants, choose exposed cliff sites to either build a nest, or merely lay and egg on the rock and sit on it. But as soon as the young are developed enough to leave, all return to the relative safety and bounty of the open sea.

The Olympic Coast National Marine Sanctuary is used by nearly 100 different species of marine birds and shorebirds. Many of the birds that are here in significant numbers in the summer time are actually not local breeders. Sooty shearwaters, one of the most abundant birds found during the summer, have colonies off South America and Australia/New

Zealand but many spend their "winter" in the eastern North Pacific. Black-footed albatross, our most common albatross, nest in the central and West Pacific (Hawaii and Japan) but many juveniles spend their formative years cruising relatively near our offshore waters. Northern fulmars breed much further north in places like the Pribiloff Islands and the Alaskan Peninsula yet are a common sight in the offshore regions of the sanctuary.

Common murres nesting on cliff. Photo credit: Olympic Coast National Marine Sanctuary.

Northern fulmar. Photo credit: Steve Lonhart, NOAA Monterey Bay National Marine Sanctuary.

Not all coastal birds are truly pelagic. Waves of thousands upon thousands of migrating shorebirds use the coastline like a road map. Their stop-off sites are few and far between yet critical to the success of their migration. Shorebirds and other migrating birds like waterfowl need to congregate in sheltered areas with abundant food to fuel their journeys. Loons, grebes and ducks abandon their freshwater breeding grounds in the late summer and often spend their winters in the nearshore ocean environment. Bald eagle, osprey and peregrine falcon nests dot the coastline, as the parent birds take full advantage of the abundance of fish and birds to feed their young. These birds, though not truly pelagic, are inextricably woven into the fabric of the ocean tapestry.

Bald Eagle. Photo credit: Carrie Vonderhaar, Ocean Futures Society.

Emerging Environmental Issues

DERELICT FISHING GEAR

Derelict fishing gear consists of nets, lines, crab/shrimp pots and other recreational or commercial fishing equipment that have been lost, abandoned or discarded in the marine environment. Derelict gear can persist in the environment for decades, killing species that encounter the gear. It is a major problem worldwide and has been identified as one of the most biologically threatening types of marine debris. Derelict gear poses a threat to marine mammals, seabirds, shellfish and fish through "ghost fishing," where the gear can attract, trap and kill a wide variety of animals. This can attract other feeding animals to perpetuate the cycle. Such wasteful killing can continue for decades.

Abandoned crab pot, in good condition and still fishing. Photo credit: Olympic Coast National Marine Sanctuary.

Ghost fishing reduces fishery stocks otherwise available for commercial and recreational fishers. Significant accumulations of gear can reduce available spawning and rearing habitat necessary to support future generations. Additionally, an abandoned net or pot can create a hazard on which other gear snags. Derelict fishing gear also can pose a threat to human safety, restrict other legitimate sanctuary uses, such as regulated fishing, anchoring and operation of vessels, and diminish the aesthetic qualities of activities such as scuba diving.

An abandoned canoe and fishing gear rest on the beach in the harbor of Neah Bay. Photo credit: Carrie Vonderhaar, Ocean Futures Society.

The extreme weather conditions and complex seabed features of the Olympic Coast National Marine Sanctuary increase the potential for fishing gear entanglement and loss. Although the area has been subjected to substantial fishing effort over the years, very little effort has been devoted to surveying and removing derelict gear or assessing its impacts on local marine resources. Sanctuary staff has observed derelict gear in the course of remotely-operated vehicle surveys of the sanctuary. In addition, there is anecdotal information about widespread derelict gear, some of which has been reported as an imminent threat to marine mammals.

Jeff,[2] a marine biologist, former crab fisher-men and commercial diver, explains to Hol-ly[3] what the Derelict Gear Removal Project has done to date. "In the last two-and-half years…we've removed over 45 tons of der-elict fishing gear…We've uncovered some 83 acres of seabed…We've also removed over a thousand crab pots and released over 1,200 crabs out of those crab pots that would've eventually died…So we've been very effec-tive but we still have a long way to go. We still have over 3,500 derelict gear targets that we haven't even looked at yet."

Dead bird in a derelict net. Photo credit: Olympic Coast National Marine Sanctuary .

Some estimates made by the Washington Department of Fish and Wildlife for areas of inner Puget Sound found that derelict fishing gear can kill up to eight percent of the population each year, Jeff explained. "That's more than our commercial and sport fisheries are taking."

---

2   Jeff June, the contractor for Derelict Fishing Gear Removal Project
3   Holly Lohuis, Education/Research Associate, Ocean Futures Society

Doing a great service to the ocean, Bet-Sea is on a mission to remove ghost nets from these waters. Photo credit: Carrie Vonderhaar, Ocean Futures Society

Onboard the Bet-Sea, Jeff doesn't hold back his enthusiasm about the Derelict Gear Removal Project and a new approach to eliminating a killer he feels has been at large too long. "We're using local harvest divers…the Tribe is assisting us with providing logistics and support…so it's a whole community based approach. We rely on fishermen and divers to tell where the gear is, then acoustic sonar to scan large areas of the seabed…Nets and pots show up as targets on the sidescan. It's a marriage of high-tech equipment and a low-tech approach." Jeff explains that it's difficult and expensive work and most of the small coastal communities don't have the resources to remove the nets like the one strung across the entrance to Neah Bay. "That's why we're here," he says.

Ocean Futures Society films the removal of derelict fishing gear, part of a collaborative conservation project in Neah Bay. Photo credit: Carrie Vonderhaar, Ocean Futures Society.

In 2005, Olympic Coast National Marine Sanctuary was awarded funds from the National Oceanic and Atmospheric Administration's Office of Restoration and Response for a pilot project to identify and remove derelict fishing gear in the northern part of the sanctuary, as well as to develop safe operating protocols for gear removal operations while working in the open ocean environment. The pilot project, a partnership with the Makah Tribe and the Northwest Straits Commission, had as its goal to build capacity in an affected community to conduct future derelict gear removal projects using resident commercial diving expertise and local people and vessels. In 2005, divers removed a particularly harmful net near the entrance to Neah Bay, in which were entangled and dead harbor seals, birds, and large fish. Several crab pots were also removed from the marina and the bay. Numerous dead and living crabs were found in these abandoned pots.

Ocean Future Society's marine biologist, Holly Lohuis picks through the algal growth on this ghost net, removing the still-living crabs and returning them to the sea. Photo credit: Carrie Vonderhaar, Ocean Futures Society.

The visibility under water quickly drops to near zero and the hardhat divers will be working blind at this point, feeling for their lift bags, attaching them to the nets in sections and gently filling them with air from a secondary air source to lightly raise the mass off the bottom. Then it's up to the ship's winch operator to gently reel in the hundreds of pounds of recovered gear. When the nets and pots reach the deck, Jeff and his team go through them to identify and log all the organisms. Anything living is returned to the sea; anything dead—fish, birds, mammals—is saved for specimen collections. This macabre inventory gives fisheries biologists an appraisal of the nets' killing power. Holly, who has researched the impact of ghost nets, is still shaken by the experience of diving on one. Her expression upon surfacing speaks volumes more than her quiet words. "The visibility was really poor, we didn't see the harbor seal until we made a second pass on the net. If we hadn't already known about it, we could have been entangled too. The harbor seal pup was only in 20 feet (6 meters) of water…If only the seal had come up a second earlier for its breath it might have missed the net altogether. It's really a tragic loss of life."

A headless harbor seal pup is among the victims of a ghost net.
Photo credit: Carrie Vonderhaar, Ocean Futures Society.

Jeff explains what happens with a gillnet that becomes lost beneath the sea. "It's almost invisible underwater to these animals and as they chase small prey species… the bait fish can swim through the mesh of the net, but the seabirds and marine mammals can't, so as they're following their prey, and unbeknownst to them, they're going to encounter this net and become entangled in it.

"We're only seeing the damage this net has done in the last two weeks but we know that it's been here for two years, so you can imagine the number of animals by multiplying what we see today by fifty or one hundred times and that's what this net has done." Jeff counts the mortalities, "Two spotted harbor seals, three grebes…What we saw today is a snapshot of what this net has been doing this past two years down there, every minute of every day. As you can see from this pile of bones, these were animals that were probably caught last month because the bones will deteriorate fairly rapidly… The harbor seal skull, several Cabazon (fish) skulls, and two bird skulls represent something that happened several weeks ago. The fresh animals we saw represent animals that have been in the net probably for less than a week."

A fish swims through a hole in an algae-covered derelict fishing net. Photo credit: Carrie Vonderhaar, Ocean Futures Society.

In 2006 and 2007, a total of three gill nets, one purse-seine/trawl net, and two commercial crab pots were removed from the water. The nets contained a total of 68 dead marine mammals (harbor seals, harbor porpoise, and sea lion), six dead seabirds (cormorants and loons), eight dead rockfish, and numerous dead crab. A crab pot that was not equipped with legal escape cord was actively fishing and contained three dead Dungeness crab.

Dungeness crab. Photo credit: Olympic Coast National Marine Sanctuary.

Research Within the Sanctuary

Olympic Coast National Marine Sanctuary conducts, or supports in partnership, several research projects including:

- Searching for deep-sea cold-water sponges and corals, and finding submerged cultural resources such as shipwrecks or ancient habitations.
- Documenting the distribution and abundance of marine mammals and seabirds off the Washington Coast and to collect and relate associated oceanographic information.
- Gathering data on seabird mortality using volunteer citizen scientists
- Investigating how quickly the seafloor recovers from disturbance. After the laying of a fiber optic cable through the sanctuary, researchers have examined the trench annually to record which organisms return and how quickly it takes them to reestablish their numbers.
- Integrating video data collected from remotely-operated vehicles (ROV) or camera sleds, bathymetry data, sedimentary samples, and other sonar mapping techniques in order to describe geological and biological aspects of habitat.
- Monitoring dissolved oxygen in order to determine the timing, severity, and extent of depleted oxygen levels along the Olympic Coast.

Researcher collecting deep sea samples from the remotely-operated vehicle. Photo credit: Olympic Coast National Marine Sanctuary.

Visiting the Sanctuary

Note: In the last section of the book, "When You Visit the Sanctuaries," is detailed information about resources found within each sanctuary to help visitors have an enjoyable and productive visit.

VISITOR'S CENTERS

Visitors can learn more about sanctuary resources, science and conservation, and opportunities to explore this wilderness coast by visiting the Olympic Coast Discovery Center in Port Angeles, and the Makah Museum in Neah Bay.

Maritime heritage exhibit.
Photo credit: Olympic Coast
National Marine Sanctuary.

Olympic Coast Discovery Center

NOAA's Olympic Coast National Marine Sanctuary
The Landing
115 East Railroad
Port Angeles, WA 98362

Open daily
10 a.m. – 5 p.m.
Admission is free.
Telephone: 360-452-3255

Trained Discovery Center staff provide detailed information on where to hike, where to see whales, where to find the best views or the most secluded beaches in the sanctuary. Exhibits and displays showcase the Olympic Coast's marine mammals, seabirds and habitats, including tidepools and deep sea canyons. Visitors can learn about the history of exploration of the Olympic Coast and the many tools that researchers use to understand the underwater landscapes, living communities and ocean processes that make Olympic Coast National Marine Sanctuary an ecological treasure. Underwater videos narrated by sanctuary researchers play in the Deepworker Theater. Educational exhibits feature the cultural heritage of the Olympic Coast region.

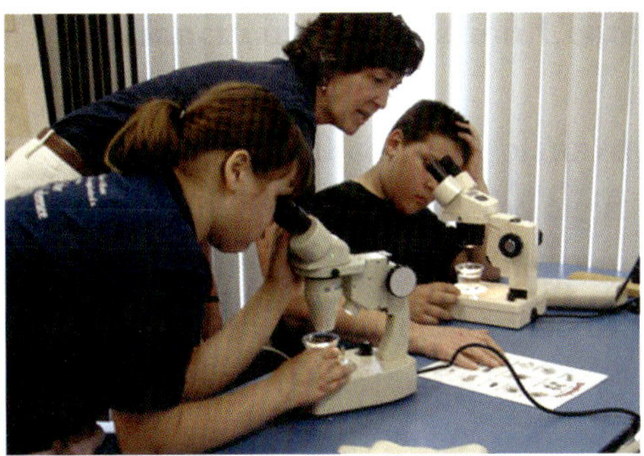

Teacher and students take a closer look using microscopes.
Photo credit: Olympic Coast National Marine Sanctuary.

Makah Cultural and Research Museum

Hwy. 112 & Bay View Ave
(P.O. Box 160)
Neah Bay, WA 98357

Open daily
10 a.m. – 5 p.m.
Closed New Year's Day, Thanksgiving and Christmas. The museum may also be closed
due to harsh weather.
Admission: There is a small admission charge.[4]
Telephone: 360-645-2711

The permanent gallery exhibits 300–500 year old artifacts recovered from a Makah village
at Ozette, Washington. There are 18 showcases, 3 dioramas and full-sized replicas of canoes
and a longhouse. The showcases interpret Makah culture and history through artifacts, text
and photographs.

---

4   http://www.makah.com/hours.html

Sanctuary administrative office location

Port Angeles Office

Olympic Coast National Marine Sanctuary

115 East Railroad Ave Suite 301

Port Angeles, WA 98362

Telephone: 360-457-6622

From kayaking to camping to wildlife watching, the Olympic Coast National Marine Sanctuary allows visitors to experience the ocean in a plethora of ways. Visitors could spend the afternoon beachcombing or watching marine wildlife, including sea otters, whales, sea lions, and birds, and then spend the night camping at Olympic National Park and Washington State Parks coastal sites. Charter fishing for salmon, rockfish, and bottomfish is also available as is recreational diving, snorkeling and kayaking. More kinds of kelp are found at the sanctuary than anywhere else in the world. A visitor can also choose to backpack on the wilderness coast, hike on the Makah Indian Reservation, or go tidepooling. There are so many ways for visitors to appreciate all different aspects of the sanctuary while protecting the area that is home to thousands of different species.

Northern fur seal. Photo credit: Olympic Coast National Marine Sanctuary.

To report a stranded marine mammal, notify the nearest State Park or National Park Ranger Station or call Olympic Coast National Marine Sanctuary at 360-457-6622, extension 13.

ECO-TOURS

Hiking along the beach. Photo credit: Olympic Coast National Marine Sanctuary.

Birding and whale watching are very rewarding throughout the year along the coast. In addition, elk and other forest wildlife are common in Olympic National Park. Regular beach walks and evening programs are offered through Olympic National Park at Kalaloch and Mora campgrounds.

Olympic Coast National Marine Sanctuary occasionally teams up with other partners for Coast Quest[5] courses. These courses for selected young people emphasize basic outdoor skills including seamanship or backpacking and add a strong mix of ocean science and marine biology. Offerings are extremely limited.

Sanctuary visitors can sign up for an Olympic Coast Learning Adventure course through Olympic Park Institute.[6] These expert-led classes for 10 to 20 participants often start at Olympic Park Institute's Lake Crescent campus and end up on the coast.

Learning around the campfire.
Photo credit: Olympic Coast National Marine Sanctuary.

5　http://olympiccoast.noaa.gov/education/featured_program/welcome.html
6　http://www.naturebridge.org/olympic-park

FISHING

Sport-fishing charters for salmon, halibut, ling cod and occasionally, albacore tuna, are available from Neah Bay, Sekiu, La Push and Westport.

Decimation of razor clam populations due to pathogen infestations and other natural calamities in the early 1980's has ended commercial harvests, but recreational digging on Washington's outer coast currently accounts for over 70% of the contiguous US coastal sport harvest. Fall, winter and spring low tides are popular for razor clamming.

Razor clams. Photo credit: Olympic Coast National Marine Sanctuary.

Fishing and shellfish gathering are regulated and licenses are required.[7]

DIVING/SNORKELING

A few dive charter operators serve the Olympic Coast—in general, ocean conditions and isolation require advanced skills and exposed, open-water experience. The Washington outer coast is known for its rough seas and large waves. Extreme waves ranging in height from 50 ft (15m) to 90 ft (29 m) have been recorded on and beyond the continental shelf.

Large crashing wave. Photo credit: Olympic Coast National Marine Sanctuary.

---

7   http://wdfw.wa.gov/fishing/regulations/

BOATING, KAYAKING and SURFING

Active water sports include sea kayaking and surfing. Cold water and local wave and current conditions pose great hazards, so skill, experience and good judgment are necessary. The Olympic Coast National Marine Sanctuary protects thick forests of kelp, home to a wide variety of animals such as seabirds, sea otters and seals. When paddling through the kelp forest, please remember that many of these animals are easily frightened. Keeping far enough away so as not to impact the animals' need to rest, feed or breed is part of a good environmental ethic and will ensure that other paddlers can have a unique wildlife encounter as well.

Kayakers in Port Angeles, Washington. Photo credit: Claire Fackler, NOAA National Marine Sanctuaries.

Boaters should drive slowly near sensitive habitats such as offshore islands, seastacks, islets and small coves. Boats should avoid kelp forests—one of the most biologically diverse habitats in the world—and be careful around kayaks, dive boats or surfers.

AVIATION and SHIPPING RESTRICTIONS

To protect seabirds, migratory waterfowl, endangered species and marine mammals, federal regulations prohibit harassing wildlife in the sanctuary by operating aircraft below 2,000 feet (610 km), within one nautical mile (1.1 mile/1.8 km) of the coast and offshore rocks and islands.

The sanctuary has worked with the U.S. Coast Guard to request the International Maritime Organization (IMO) designate an Area to be Avoided (ATBA) on the Olympic Coast. The ATBA is defined as "a routeing measure comprising an area within defined limits in which either navigation is particularly hazardous or it is exceptionally important to avoid casualties and which should be avoided by all ships, or certain classes of ships". This ATBA was adopted in December 1994 "in order to reduce the risk of marine casualty and resulting pollution and damage to the environment of the Olympic Coast National Marine Sanctuary." The ATBA went into effect in June 1995 and advises operators of vessels carrying petroleum and/or hazardous materials to maintain a 25-mile (40 km) buffer from the coast. Since that time, Olympic Coast National Marine Sanctuary has created an education and monitoring program with the goal of ensuring the successful implementation of the ATBA.

Sunset at the Olympic Coast National Marine Sanctuary.
Photo Credit: Carrie Vonderhaar, Ocean Futures Society.

When You Visit the Sanctuaries

Channel Islands National Marine Sanctuary

Sanctuary Offices

Santa Barbara Office

113 Harbor Way, Suite 150
Santa Barbara, CA 93109
Telephone: 805-966-7107
Fax: 805-568-1582
www.channelislands.noaa.gov

Southern Office

Channel Islands Harbor
3600 S. Harbor Blvd., Suite 2-202
Oxnard, CA. 93035
Telephone: 805-382-6149
Fax: 805-382-9791

Visitor Centers

Outdoors Santa Barbara Visitor Center

113 Harbor Way, 4th floor
Santa Barbara, CA. 93109
Telephone: 805-884-1475

The Santa Barbara Maritime Museum

113 Harbor Way
Santa Barbara, California, 93109
Telephone: 805-962-8404

Cabrillo High School Aquarium

4350 Constellation Rd.
Vandenberg Village, CA 93436
Telephone: 805-742-2888

Santa Barbara Museum of Natural History Sea Center

2559 Puesta del Sol
Santa Barbara, California 93105
Telephone: 805-682-4711

Channel Islands National Park Visitor Center

1901 Spinnaker Drive
Ventura, California 93001
Telephone: 805-658-5730

The following resources will help make your visit to the Channel Islands National Marine Sanctuary more enjoyable.

Chambers of Commerce

There are three chambers serving the Channel Islands area. Each one has specific information about services and businesses within the geographic area it serves.

Santa Barbara Chamber of Commerce

924 Anacapa Street, Suite 1
Santa Barbara, CA 93101
Telephone: 805-965-3023
Fax: 805-966-5954
Email: info@sbchamber.org
www.sbchamber.org

Chamber of Commerce Visitor Center

1 Garden Street
Santa Barbara, CA 93101
Telephone: 805-965-3021

Ventura Chamber of Commerce

505 Poli Street, Second Floor
Ventura, CA 93001
Telephone: 805-643-7222
www.ventura-chamber.org

Oxnard Chamber of Commerce

400 E. Esplanade Drive, Suite 302
Oxnard, CA 93036
Telephone: 805-983-6118
Fax: 805-604-7331
Email: info@oxnardchamber.org
www.oxnardchamber.org

Map

SANTA BARBARA COUNTY
Santa Barbara
VENTURA COUNTY
Point Conception
Santa Barbara Channel
Ventura
Oxnard
NOAA
NATIONAL OCEANIC AND ATMOSPHERIC ADMINISTRATION
U.S. DEPARTMENT OF COMMERCE
NATIONAL MARINE SANCTUARIES
LOS ANGELES COUNTY
San Miguel
Santa Rosa
Santa Cruz
Anacapa
Los Angeles
Long Beach
Channel Islands National Marine Sanctuary
N
0 5 10 20 Miles
0 5 10 20 Kilometers
Channel Islands National Marine Sanctuary
Marine Protected Areas Network
Established in 2003 and 2007
Marine Reserve
Marine Conservation Area
Marine Conservation Area
Santa Barbara
San Nicolas
Santa Catalina
San Clemente

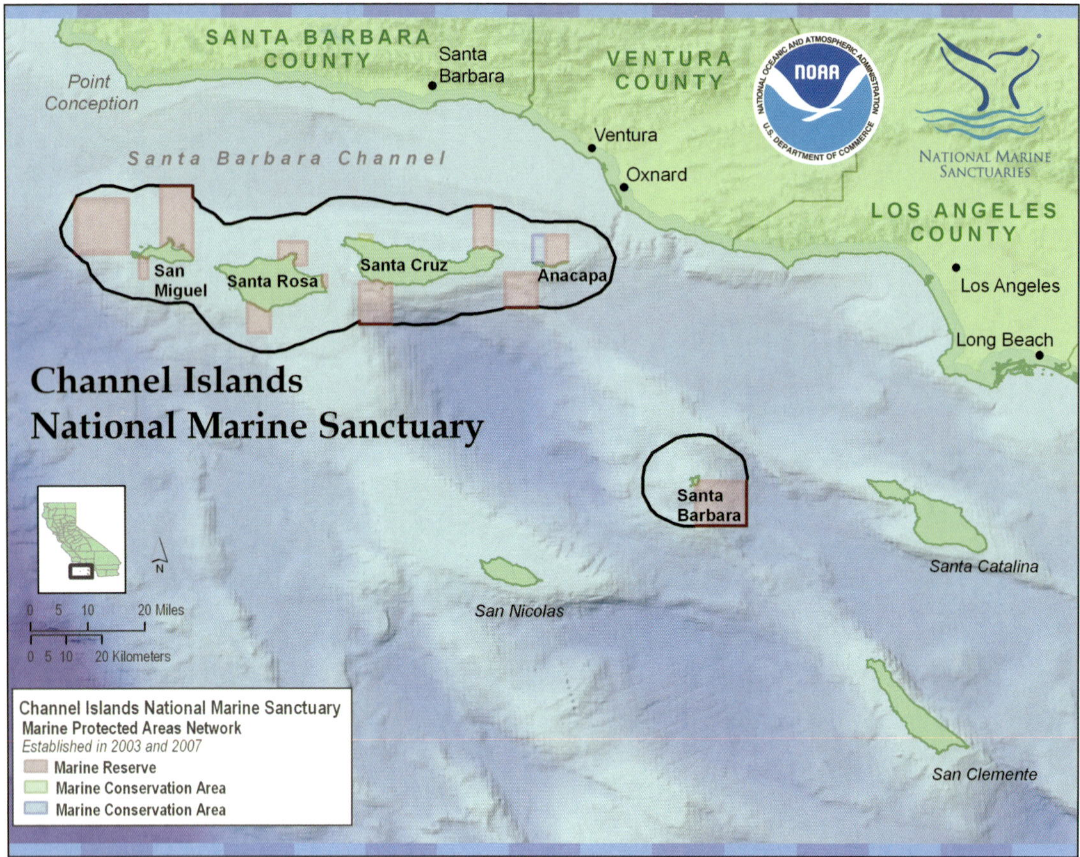

Air and Ground Transportation

The major aviation gateway to the Channel Islands area is Los Angeles International Airport (LAX, www.lawa.org/welcomelax.aspx), with three other airports providing either commercial or general aviation services.

> Los Angeles International Airport
> 1 World Way
> Los Angeles, CA 90045
> Telephone: 310-646-5252
> www.lawa.org/welcomelax.aspx

Most major international airlines and many smaller regional carriers fly into Los Angeles International Airport. Visit www.lawa.org/welcomelax.aspx for full details of all available carriers and flights.

Rental Cars

Rental car agencies at the airport include Advantage, Alamo, Avis, Budget, Dollar, Enterprise, Hertz, Fox, Payless, National, and Thrifty, all of which may be found at www.lawa.org/welcome_lax.aspx?id=1294 or at their respective corporate web sites.

Taxi

Taxi service is provided by nine different companies, which may be found at www.lawa.org/welcome_lax.aspx?id=942.

Bus/Shuttle

Bus and shuttle service to the metropolitan area is provided by eight bus companies, which may be found at www.lawa.org/welcome_lax.aspx?id=1296.

Santa Barbara Municipal Airport (SBA, www.flysba.com)

Santa Barbara Municipal Airport
500 Fowler Road
Santa Barbara, CA 93117
Telephone: 805-681-4803
www.flysba.com

This airport has five commercial airlines providing scheduled flights and two fixed base operators providing fuel, maintenance and related aircraft services. There are two snack bars, a restaurant, four rental car agencies, numerous taxi companies and two shuttle services.

Scheduled Commercial Airlines

Alaska
Toll Free: 800-252-7522

American
Toll Free: 800-433-7300

Frontier
Toll Free: 800-432-1359

United
Toll Free: 800-864-8331

US Airways
Toll Free: 800-428-4322

Aircraft Services

Atlantic Aviation
Telephone: 805-964-6733

Signature Flight Support
Telephone: 805-967-5608

Rental Cars

Budget
Telephone: 805-964-6792

Enterprise
Telephone: 805-683-3012

Hertz
Telephone: 805-967-0411

National
Telephone: 805-967-1202

Taxi Cab Companies

American Taxi
Telephone: 805-689-0683

Crown Cab
Telephone: 805-689-0234

Fly By Night Taxi
Telephone: 805-886-8617

Roadways Cab
Telephone: 805-683-6200

Rose Cab
Telephone: 805-451-0426

Santa Barbara Airport Taxi
 Telephone: 805-895-2422 (not affiliated with the airport)

Santa Barbara City Cab
 Telephone: 805-968-6868

Santa Barbara Checker Cab
Telephone: 805-560-8284

Santa Barbara Yellow Cab
Telephone: 805-965-5111

Shuttle

Central Coast Shuttle
Telephone: 805-928-1977

Road Runner
Telephone: 805-389-8196

Oxnard Airport (OXR, www.iflyoxnard.com)

> Oxnard Airport
> 2889 W. Fifth Street
> Oxnard, CA 93030

Oxnard Airport is a general aviation airport with four rental car agencies, two fixed base operators, fuel, maintenance, and taxi service, but there is not a restaurant.

Aircraft Services:

> Golden West Jet Center
> Telephone: 805-382-9333

> Oxnard Jet Center
> Telephone: 805-985-2490

Rental Cars

> Budget
> Telephone: 805-382-8351

> Dollar
> Telephone: 805-984-7870

> Enterprise
> Telephone: 805-985-8888

> Hertz
> Telephone: 805-985-0911

Taxi

Yellow Cab
Telephone: 805-659-6900

Shuttle (To and From LAX)

Amadeus Limousine & Shuttle
Telephone: 805-486-1873

Roadrunner Shuttle
Toll Free: 800-247-7919

Ventura County Airporter & Limousine
Telephone: 805-650-6600

Camarillo Airport (CMA, www.portal.countyofventura.org/portal/page/portal/airports/
Camarillo%20Airport)

555 Airport Way
Camarillo, CA 93010
Telephone: 805-388-4274

Located inland from the coast and about half-way between Santa Barbara and Los Angeles,
Camarillo Airport is a general aviation facility with typical services, including fixed base
operators, fuel, maintenance, hangars, ground transportation and one restaurant.

Aircraft Services

Avantair Elite Services
Telephone: 805-383-1100

Channel Island Aviation
Telephone: 805-9871301

Sun Air Jets
Telephone: 805-389-9301

Western Cardinal Air
Telephone: 805-482-2586

Rental Cars

Enterprise
Available through Western Cardinal Air and Sun Air Jets (see Aircraft Services above)

Hertz
Available through Channel Island Aviation (see Aircraft Services above)

Taxi

Gold Coast Cab
Telephone: 805-850-5054

Thousand Oaks Cab
Telephone: 805-495-3500

Yellow Cab
Telephone: 805-384-9325

Shuttle

Camarillo Airport Limo Services
Toll Free: 866-546-6726

Roadrunner Shuttle and Limo
Toll Free: 800-247-7919

Accommodations, restaurants, markets, and attractions

Because of the wide variety of commercial enterprises available to the public, we recommend that visitors check with area chambers of commerce for lists of local businesses in all categories, from where to stay to where to eat and what to do.

Diving Operations

There are many diving operations in the Channel Islands area, among them are:

CalBoat Diving
Ventura Harbor
Ventura, CA
Toll Free: 866-225-3483
Telephone: 805-486-1166

Channel Islands Dive Adventures
Telephone: 805-469-7288
Email: info@channelislandsdiveadventures.com
www.channelislandsdiveadventures.com

Channel Islands Scuba
3200 E. Thousand Oaks Blvd.

Thousand Oaks, CA. 91362
Telephone: 805-230-9995
Fax: 805-230-9978
Email: info@cisdivers.com
www.cisdivers.com

SoCal Dive
Channel Islands Harbor
3600 Harbor Blvd 219
Oxnard, CA 93035
Telephone: 805-204-0977
Email: info@socaldive.com
www.socaldive.com

Truth Aquatics
301 West Cabrillo Boulevard
Santa Barbara, CA 93101
Telephone: 805-962-1127
www.truthaquatics.com/index.html

Fishing Charters

Fishing charter companies can be found throughout the Channel Islands area. Here are just a few:

Channel Islands Sportfishing Center
4151 S. Victoria Avenue
Oxnard, CA 93035
Telephone: 805-382-1612
www.channelislandssportfishing.com

Fuji Charters
1404 Anchors Way, Ventura Harbor
Ventura, CA 93003
Telephone: 805-815-7655
Email: captain@fujicharters.com
www.fujicharters.com

Hook's Landing Sportfishing
3550 South Harbor Blvd, Suite 2-105
Oxnard, CA 93035
Telephone: 805-382-6233
Email: info@hookslanding.net
www.hookslanding.net

Whale Watching

There are several companies providing whale watching cruises to the Channel Islands. A few are:

Channel Islands Sportfishing Center
4151 S. Victoria Avenue
Oxnard, CA 93035
Telephone: 805-382-1612
www.channelislandssportfishing.com

Condor Cruises
301 W. Cabrillo Blvd.
Santa Barbara, CA 93109
Toll Free: 888-779-4253
Telephone: 805-882-0088

Island Packers
1691 Spinnaker Dr.
Ventura, CA 93001
Telephone: 805-642-1393
www.islandpackers.com

Remember, if you can't find what you are looking for in these pages, contact the local area chamber of commerce for help. Even if they don't know the answer to your question, they will find it for you. Enjoy your Sanctuary visit.

Monterey Bay National Marine Sanctuary

SANCTUARY OFFICES

Monterey Office:

299 Foam Street
Monterey, CA 93940
Telephone: 831-647-4201
Email: montereybay@noaa.gov
www.montereybay.noaa.gov/welcome.html

San Simeon Office:

Hearst Memorial State Beach
P.O. Box 116
San Simeon, CA 93452
Telephone: 805-927-2145

Santa Cruz Office

110 Shaffer Road
Santa Cruz, CA 95060
Telephone: 831-420-3663

Visitor Centers

Coastal Discovery Center

Building 1 Hearst State Beach at San Luis Obispo
San Simeon Road
San Simeon, CA 93452
Telephone: 805-927-6575
www.coastaldiscoverycenter.org

Sanctuary Exploration Center (Santa Cruz)

This 12,000 center is planned to open in 2012 and contain exhibits, classrooms, administrative space and a gift shop. Current funding remains short of the needed amount to complete the project. For more information visit: http://www.nmsfocean.org/campaign/monterey-bay-national-marine-sanctuary-exploration-center-santa-cruz.

The following resources will help make your visit to the Channel Islands National Marine Sanctuary more enjoyable.

Chambers of Commerce

Monterey Peninsula Chamber of Commerce
30 Ragsdale Drive, Suite 200
Monterey, CA 93940
Telephone: 831-648-5360
Fax: 831-649-3502
Email: info@mpcc.com
www.mpcc.com

Pacific Grove Chamber of Commerce
584 Central Avenue
Pacific Grove, CA 93950
Toll Free: 800-656-6650
Telephone: 831-373-3304
Fax: 831-373-3317
chamber@pacificgrove.org
www.pacificgrove.org

Map

123°0'W
122°0'W
121°0'W
Gulf of the Farallones
National Marine
Sanctuary
NOAA
NATIONAL MARINE
SANCTUARIES
MONTEREY BAY
0   10   20   30
Miles
San Francisco
Half Moon Bay
Santa Cruz
Monterey Bay
National Marine
Sanctuary
Monterey Canyon
Monterey
37°0'N
36°0'N
Monterey Bay
National Marine
Sanctuary
Davidson Seamount
San Simeon
Cambria
123°0'W
122°0'W
121°0'W

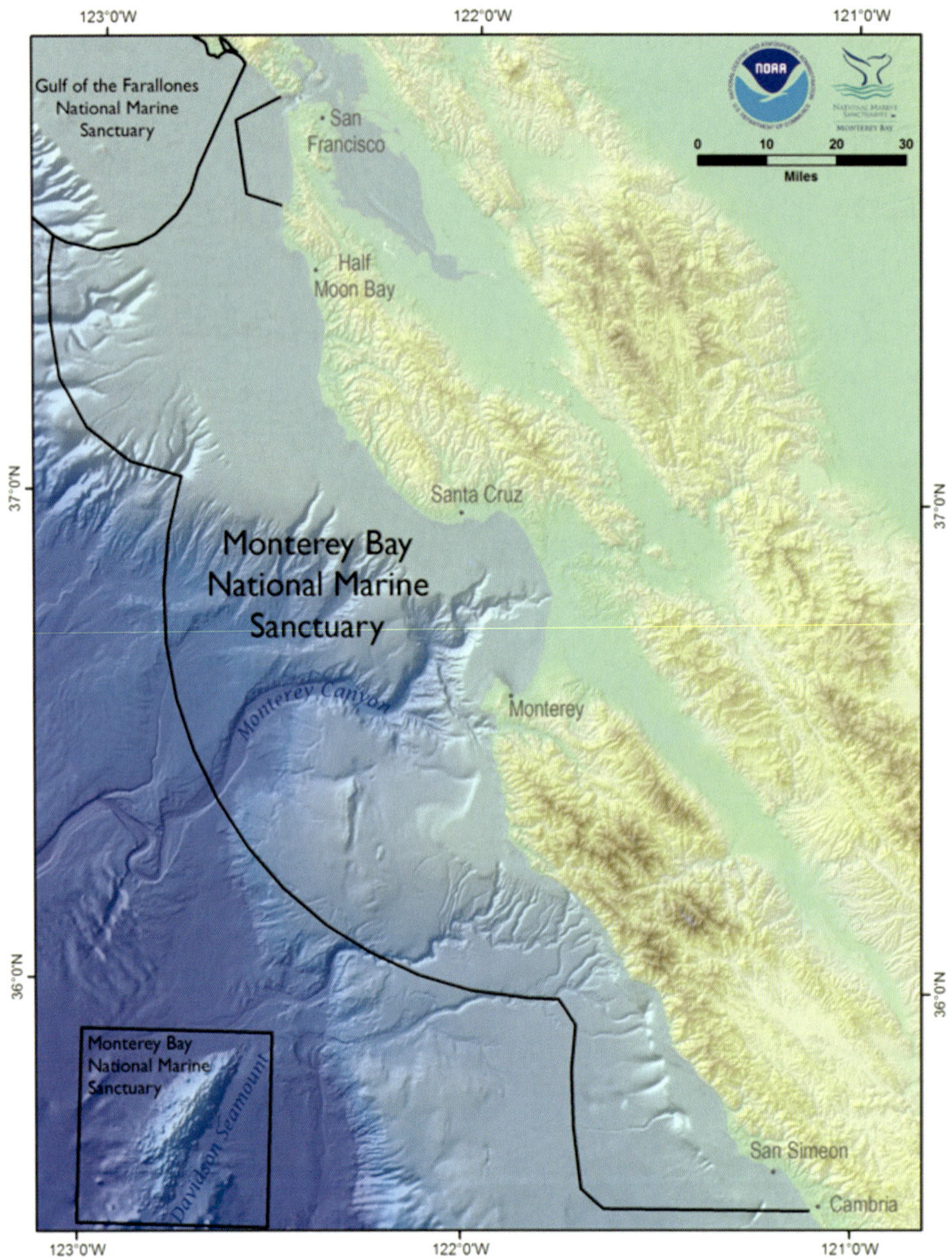

Air and Ground Transportation

The **Monterey Peninsula Airport** (MRY, http://www.montereyairport.com) provides commercial and private aircraft access to the Monterey area.

Scheduled Commercial Airlines

> Allegiant
> Telephone: 702-505-8888

> America Eagle
> Toll Free: 800-433-7300

> United Express
> Toll Free: 800-241-6522

> US Airways
> Toll Free: 800-428-4322

Aircraft Services

> Del Monte Aviation
> Telephone: 831-373-4151

> Monterey Bay Aviation
> Telephone: 831-375-2359

> Monterey Jet Center
> Telephone: 831-373-0100

Rental Cars

Alamo
Toll Free: 800-327-9633

Avis
Toll Free: 800-831-2847

Budget
Toll Free: 800-527-0700

Enterprise
Toll Free: 800-736-8222

Hertz
Toll Free: 800-654-3131

National
Toll Free: 800-227-7368

Taxi Cab

Central Coast Taxi
Telephone: 831-626-3333

Bus

Monterey Salinas Transit
Telephone: 831-899-2555

Accommodations, Restaurants, Markets, and Attractions

Because of the wide variety of commercial enterprises available to the public, we recommend that visitors check with area Chambers of Commerce for lists of local businesses in all categories, from where to stay to where to eat and what to do.

Diving Operations

Beside many shore-based entry points, the Sanctuary provides some of the best diving opportunities on the West Coast. A few dive operators are:

Aquarius Dive Shop
Bruce Sawyer
2040 Del Monte Ave.
Monterey, CA 93940
Telephone: 831-375-1933
Email: aquariusds@sbcglobal.net
www.aquariusdivers.com

Glenn's Aquarius II Dive Shop
32 Cannery Row
Monterey, CA 93940
Toll Free: 866-375-6605
Telephone: 831-375-6605
Fax: 831-657-1024
Email: dive@aquarius2.com
www.dive@aquarius2.com

Monterey Bay Dive Charters
Jim Fields
100 Cannery Row

Monterey, CA 93940
Telephone: 831-383-9276
Email: info@mbdcscuba.com
www.mbdcscuba.com/index.htm

Fishing Charters

Recreational fishing is a favorite activity in the Sanctuary because of the variety of different species. Some fishing charters are:

Chris' Fishing Trips
48 Fisherman's Wharf #1
Monterey, CA 93940
Telephone: 831-375-5951
Email: chris4fish@aol.com

Randy's Fishing and Whale Watching Trips
Peter Bruno
66 Fisherman's Wharf
Monterey, CA 93940
Toll Free: 800-251-7440
Telephone: 831-372 - 7440
Fax: 831-372 - 7442
www.randysfishingtrips.com

Westwind Charter Sport Fishing & Excursions
7881 Sandholt Rd. B-Dock
Moss Landing, CA 95039
Telephone: 831-392-7867
Email: westwind@charter.net

Whale Watching

California is one of the few places in the world where visitors can see whales year-round and can sometimes be seen from shore with the naked eye. Some whale watch operations are:

Monterey Bay Whale Watch
Fisherman's Wharf #1
Monterey, CA 93940
Telephone: 831-375-4658
Email: whaletrips@gowhales.com
www.montereybaywhalewatch.com

Princess Monterey Whale Watching Cruises
96 Fisherman's Wharf #1
Monterey, CA 93940
Toll Free:800-200-2203
Telephone: 831-372-2203
www.montereywhalewatching.com

Randy's Fishing Trips
66 Fisherman's Wharf #1
Monterey, CA 93940
Toll Free: 800-251-7440
Telephone: 831-372-7440
www.randysfishingtrips.com

Sanctuary Cruises
7881 Sandholdt Road
Moss Landing, CA 95039
Telephone: 831-917-1042

mike@sanctuarycruises.com
www.sanctuarycruises.com

Sailing

Sailboat charters and schools are readily available in the area. Below are two operators to consider:

Carrera Sailing

66 Fisherman's Wharf
Monterey, CA 93940
Telephone: 831-375-0648
Email: captaingene@sailmontereybay.com
www.sailmontereybay.com

Monterey Bay Sailing

78 Old Fisherman's Wharf #1
Monterey, CA 93940
Telephone: 831-372-7245
Email: capt_dutch@montereysailing.com
www.montereysailing.com

Remember, if you can't find what you are looking for in these pages, contact the local area chamber of commerce for help. Even if they don't know the answer to your question, they will find it for you. Enjoy your Sanctuary visit.

Gulf of the Farallones National Marine Sanctuary

Sanctuary Office

991 Marine Drive, The Presidio
San Francisco, CA 94129
Telephone: 415-561-6622
Fax: 415-561-6616
Email: farallones@noaa.gov
www.farallones.noaa.gov

Visitor Center

Gulf of the Farallones NMS Visitor Center
991 Marine Drive, The Presidio
San Francisco, CA 94129
Telephone: 415-561-6622

The following resources will help make your visit to the Gulf of the Farallones National Marine Sanctuary more enjoyable.

Chamber of Commerce

San Francisco Chamber of Commerce
235 Montgomery Street, 12th Floor
San Francisco, CA 94104
Telephone: 415-392-4520
www.sfchamber.com/chamber

West Marin Chamber of Commerce
P.O. Box 1045
Point Reyes Station, CA 94956
Telephone: 415-663-9232
Email: info@pointreyes.org
www.pointreyes.org

Map

Bodega Head
Sonoma County
Napa County
Solano County
Cordell Bank
National Marine Sanctuary
Marin County
San Pablo Bay
Drakes Bay
Point Reyes
Contra Costa County
Gulf of the Farallones
National Marine Sanctuary
Farallon Islands
San Francisco
Main Office
San Francisco Bay
Alameda County
Pillar Point
Half Moon Bay
Half Moon Bay
Field Office
Santa Clara County
San Mateo County
Monterey Bay
National Marine Sanctuary
Santa Cruz County
Point Año Nuevo
N
5   10   15
Nautical Miles

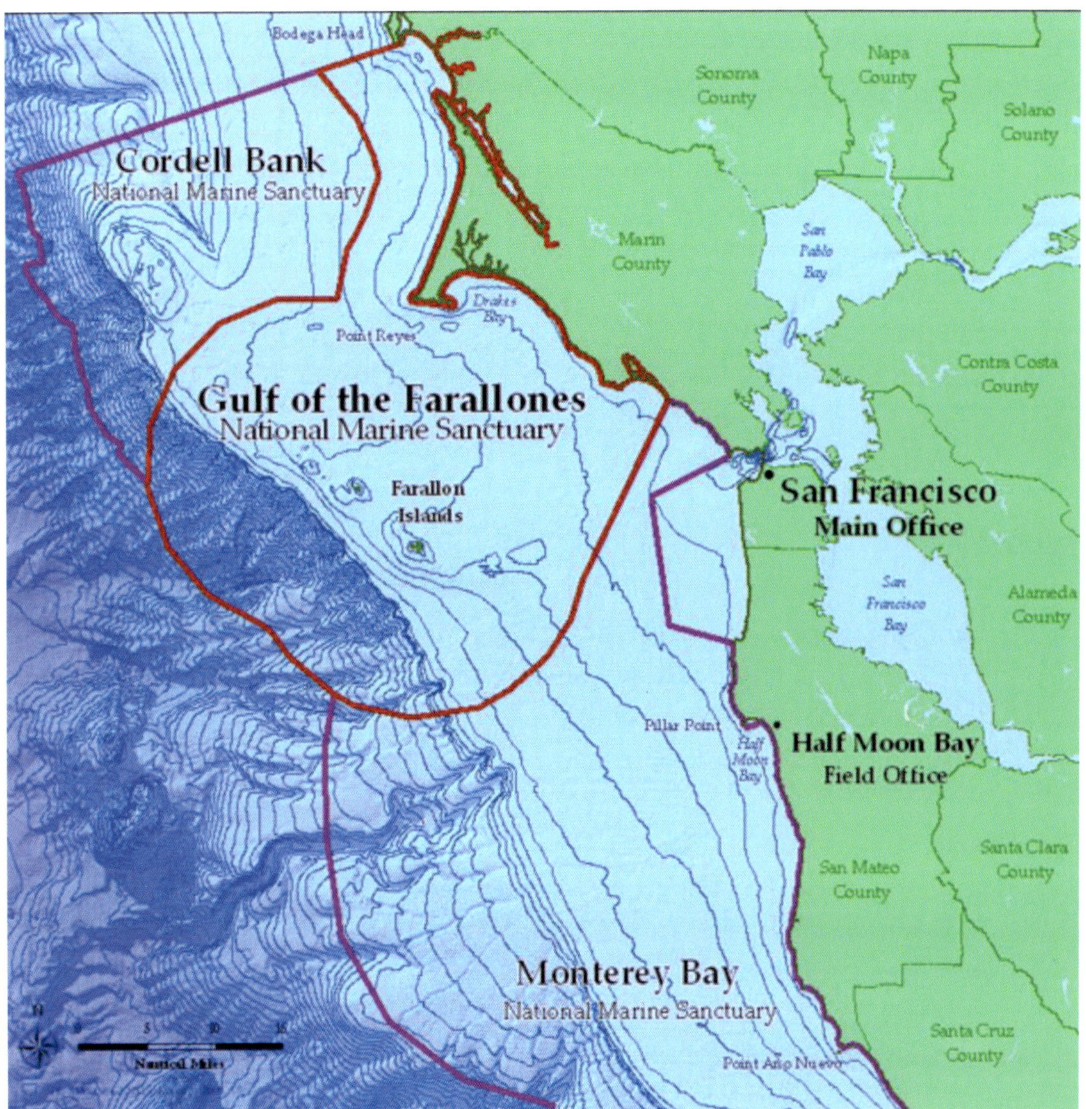

Air and Ground Transportation

The major aviation gateway to this part of California is provided through San Francisco International Airport (SFO, www.flysfo.com/web/page/index.jsp), with all major international and domestic air carriers operating scheduled flights. General aviation services are also available on site and at many civil airports within a fifty mile radius.

San Francisco International Airport
P. O. Box 8097
San Francisco, CA 94128-8097
Toll Free: 800-435-9736
Telephone: 650-821-8211
www.flysfo.com/web/page/index.jsp

Rental Cars

Rental car agencies with offices at the airport include Alamo, Avis, Budget, Dollar, Enterprise, Fox, Hertz, National and Thrifty, all of which may be found at www.flysfo.com/web/page/tofrom/rental-cars/rc-agencies
or at their respective corporate web sites.

Taxi/Shuttle

Taxi and shuttle services are also plentiful and may be found at www.flysfo.com/web/page/tofrom/transp-serv.

Accommodations, Restaurants, Markets, and Attractions

Because of the wide variety of commercial enterprises available to the public, we recommend that visitors check with area Chambers of Commerce for lists of local businesses in all categories, from where to stay to where to eat and what to do.

Diving Operations

Recreational diving is **not recommended** in the Sanctuary because of the difficult ocean conditions and the fact that the Sanctuary is a breeding ground for white sharks.

Fishing Charters

Charter fishing trips are available from the San Francisco Bay area. Among them are:

Captain Joey's
Fisherman's Wharf
San Francisco, CA
Telephone: 415-892-2353

Emeryville Sportfishing
3310 Powell Street
Emeryville, CA 94608
Toll Free: 800-575-9944
Telephone: 510-654-6040

Flash Sport Fishing
Telephone: 510-881-0858
Email: flashfishing@talcorp.net
www.flashfishing.net

Salty Lady Sport Fishing
Telephone: 415-674-3474
Email: reservations@saltylady.com
www.saltylady.com

SF Bay Adventures
1001 Bridgeway, Suite B2A
Sausalito, California 94965
Telephone: 415-331-0444
Email: info@sfbayadventures.com
www.sfbayadventures.com/farallon_islands.htm

Whale Watching

Whale watching is a favorite activity of locals and visitors to the area. Among those companies providing whale watching charters are;

California Whale Adventures
Telephone: 650-579-7777
www.californiawhaleadventures.com/index.htm

Oceanic Society
30 Sir Francis Drake Blvd.
P.O. Box 437
Ross, CA 94957
Toll Free: 800-326-7491
Telephone: 415-441-1106
Email: office@oceanicsociety.org
www.acs-sfbay.org/index.html

San Francisco Whale Tours
Toll Free: 800-979-3370
Telephone: 212-209-3370
Email: info@sanfranciscowhaletours.com
www.sanfranciscowhaletours.com

SF Bay Whale Watching

300 Napa St, Slip #26

Sausalito, CA 94965

Telephone: 415-331-6267

Email: vern@sfbaywhalewatching.com

www.sfbaywhalewatching.com

Remember, if you can't find what you are looking for in these pages, contact the local area chamber of commerce for help. Even if they don't know the answer to your question, they will find it for you. Enjoy your Sanctuary visit.

Cordell Bank National Marine Sanctuary

Sanctuary Office

Sanctuary Office
1 Bear Valley Rd.
Point Reyes Station, CA 94956

Mailing Address: PO Box 159
Olema, CA 94950
Telephone: 415-663-0314
www.cordellbank.noaa.gov/contact/welcome.html

Visitor Center

Cordell Bank **does not** have a Visitor's Center. However, visitors to the area can learn about the Sanctuary at these locations:

Pt. Reyes National Seashore Visitor Center
www.nps.gov/pore/planyourvisit/visitorcenters.htm

Gulf of the Farallones National Marine Sanctuary Visitor Center
www.farallones.noaa.gov/education/schoolprograms.html

Bodega Marine Lab, University of California-Davis
www.bml.ucdavis.edu

The following resources will help make your visit to the Cordell Bank National Marine Sanctuary more enjoyable.

Chambers of Commerce

San Francisco Chamber of Commerce
235 Montgomery Street, 12th Floor
San Francisco, CA 94104
Telephone: 415-392-4520
Fax: 415-392-0485
www.sfchamber.com

Bodega Bay Area Chamber of Commerce
P.O. Box 146
Bodega Bay, CA 94923
Telephone: 707-347-9645
Email: chamber@bodegabayca.org
www.bodegabayca.org/bodega-bay-area-chamber-of-commerce

Map

Air and Ground Transportation

The major aviation gateway to this part of California is provided through **San Francisco International Airport** (SFO, www.flysfo.com/web/page/index.jsp), with all major international and domestic air carriers operating scheduled flights. General aviation services are also available on site and at many civil airports within a fifty mile radius.

> San Francisco International Airport
> P. O. Box 8097
> San Francisco, CA 94128-8097
> Toll Free: 800-435-9736
> Telephone: 650-821-8211
> www.flysfo.com/web/page/index.jsp

Rental Cars

Rental car agencies with offices at the airport include Alamo, Avis, Budget, Dollar, Enterprise, Fox, Hertz, National and Thrifty, all of which may be found at www.flysfo.com/web/page/tofrom/rental-cars/rc-agencies
or at their respective corporate web sites.

Taxi/Shuttle

Taxi and shuttle services are also plentiful and may be found at www.flysfo.com/web/page/tofrom/transp-serv.

Accommodations, Restaurants, Markets, and Attractions

Because of the wide variety of commercial enterprises available to the public, we recommend that visitors check with area Chambers of Commerce for lists of local businesses in all categories, from where to stay to where to eat and what to do.

Diving Operations

Recreational diving is **not recommended** at Cordell Bank because of the deep water, plus strong currents that are extremely variable and can run in opposite directions at different depths. Sea conditions change rapidly, with fog and wind developing quickly. Dive conditions are treacherous.

Fishing Charters

Recreational fishing within Cordell Bank National Marine Sanctuary is closed for most species, but seasonal fishing occurs and is regulated by federal and state authorities. Fishing charters are available out of Bodega Bay, CA, but these are based on seasons, presence of authorized species, and government regulations.

Whale Watching

Commercial trips to Cordell Bank National Marine Sanctuary are not offered regularly, however, the Sanctuary co-sponsors a field seminar with Point Reyes National Seashore Association's Field Seminars Program to introduce participants to the offshore wildlife that makes Cordell Bank such a special place. More information is available at www.cordellbank.noaa.gov/visit/wildlife.html.

Shearwater Journeys
P.O. Box 190
Hollister, CA 95024
Telephone: 831-637-8527
debi@shearwaterjourneys.com
www.shearwaterjourneys.com

Remember, if you can't find what you are looking for in these pages, contact the local area chamber of commerce for help. Even if they don't know the answer to your question, they will find it for you. Enjoy your Sanctuary visit.

Olympic Coast National Marine Sanctuary

Sanctuary Office

Olympic Coast National Marine Sanctuary
115 East Railroad Ave., Suite 301
Port Angeles, WA 98362
Telephone: 360-457-6622
FAX: 360-457-8496
Email: olympiccoast@noaa.gov

Visitor Center

Olympic Coast Discovery Center
115 East Railroad
Port Angeles, WA, 98362
Telephone: 360-452-3255

Open Memorial Day through Labor Day, and by appointment. To schedule a tour call 360-457-6622 ext. 31.

The following resources will help make your visit to the Olympic Coast National Marine Sanctuary more enjoyable.

Chamber of Commerce

Port Angeles Regional Chamber of Commerce
121 E. Railroad
Port Angeles, WA 98362.
Telephone: 360-452-2363
Email: info@portangeles.org
www.portangeles.org

Map

Swiftsure Bank
Strait of Juan de Fuca
Tatoosh Island
Neah Bay
Cape Flattery
Sekiu
Clallam Bay
Nitinat Canyon
Cape Alava
Juan de Fuca Canyon
FLATTERY ROCKS NWR
La Push
QUILLAYUTE NEEDLES NWR
OLYMPIC COAST NATIONAL MARINE SANCTUARY
Destruction Island
Kalaloch
COPALIS NWR
N
W
E
S
Quinault Canyon
Taholah
Point Grenville
Moclips
Pacific Beach
Copalis Beach
300-750 meters
less than 300 meters
Olympic National Park
Indian Reservation
-1900m -1500m -1100m -800m -250m -80m -20m -5m

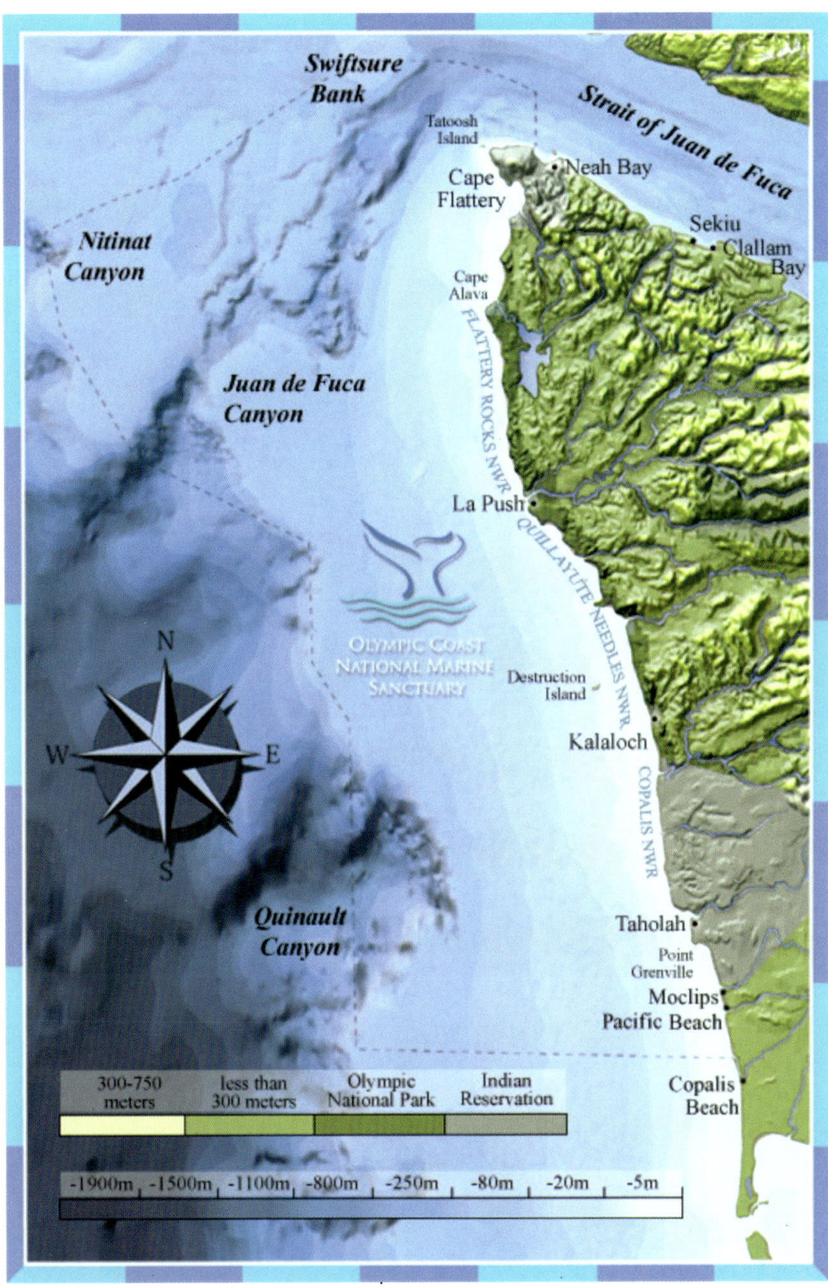

Air, Ground and Ferry Transportation

Air transportation service to the Olympic Coast area is via the Port Angeles Airport (CLM), Port Angeles, WA. The only scheduled air flights are via Kenmore Air Express, which partners with Alaska Airlines.

Kenmore Air Express
1404 West Airport Road
Port Angeles WA 98363
Toll Free: 866-435-9524 x2271
Telephone: 360-452-6371
Fax: 360-452-5607
www.kenmoreair.com

Scenic flights, charter flights, flight lessons, fuel, and aircraft maintenance are available from Rite Bros. Aviation at Port Angeles Airport.

Rite Bros Aviation
1406 Fairchild Airport Way
Port Angeles WA 98363
Toll Free: 800-430-7483
Telephone: 360-452-6226
Fax: 360-457-0386
www.ritebros.com

Monday thru Friday 8:00 a.m. to 7:30 p.m.; Saturday & Sunday 8:30 a.m. to 7:30 p.m.

Ground transportation

Rental Car

Two rental agencies are located at Port Angeles Airport:

Enterprise (360-417-3083) and Budget (360-452-4774), which also may be contacted through their corporate web sites.

Bus

Dungeness Line (To Seattle)
Toll Free: 800-457-4492
Telephone: 360-417-0700

Clallam Transit (Port Angeles)
Telephone: 360-452-1315
Fax: 360-452-1316
www.clallamtransit.com

Shuttle (To SEA-TAC Airport in Seattle)

Rocket Transportation
Toll Free: 877-697-6258
Telephone: 360-683-8087
www.gorocketman.com

Ferry Transportation (Port Angeles to/from Victoria, British Columbia, CAN)

Black Ball Ferry Line
101 E Railroad Ave
Port Angeles WA 98362
Toll Free: 877-386-2202
Telephone: 360-457-4491
Fax: 360-457-4493
www.cohoferry.com

Accommodations, Restaurants, Markets, and Attractions

Because of the wide variety of commercial enterprises available to the public, we recommend that visitors check with area Chambers of Commerce for lists of local businesses in all categories, from where to stay to where to eat and what to do.

Diving Operations

A few dive charter operators serve the Olympic Coast , however, ocean conditions and isolation require advanced skills and exposed, open-water experience.

Fishing Charters

Sport-fishing charters for salmon, halibut, ling cod and occasionally, albacore tuna, are available from Neah Bay, Sekiu, La Push and Westport. The following are just a few:

Cachalot Charters
2511 N. Westhaven Drive
Westport, WA 98595
Toll Free: 800-356-0323
Telephone: 360-268-0323
www.cachalotcharters.com

Excel Fishing Charters
Neah Bay, WA 98357
Toll Free: 877-805-1729
Telephone: 360-805-1729
www.excelfishingcharters.com

Tommycod Charters
Sekiu, WA
Toll Free: 800-283-8900
Telephone: 360-963-0759
www.tommycodcharters.com

Top Notch Ocean Charters
1933 Mora Rd.
La Push, WA 98331
Toll Free: 888-501-5887
Telephone: 360-374-2660
www.forks-web.com/jim/salt.htm

Whale Watching

A few operators provide whale watch trips, the following is just one.

Advantage Charters
P.O. Box 1991
Westport, WA 98595
Toll Free: 800- 689-5595
Telephone: 360-648-2277
fishbiz1@comcast.net

Remember, if you can't find what you are looking for in these pages, contact the local area chamber of commerce for help. Even if they don't know the answer to your question, they will find it for you. Enjoy your Sanctuary visit.

Acknowledgments

- The *Explore the National Marine Sanctuaries with Jean-Michel Cousteau* series would not be possible without the creation of the two-hour PBS television special, *America's Underwater Treasures,* co-produced with KQED Public Broadcasting in San Francisco, the companion limited edition book *America's Underwater Treasures*, and the talented people who contributed to those projects
- Julie Robinson, co-author *America's Underwater Treasures* Limited Edition Book
- The staff at Ocean Futures Society: Charles Vinick, Sandra Squires, Lida Pardisi, Laura Brands, Carey Batha, Jim Knowlton, Brian Hall, Nathan Dembeck, Matthew Ferraro, Carrie Vonderhaar, Nancy Marr, Marie-Claude Oren
- Ocean Futures Society's Dr. Richard Murphy, Director of Science and Education; Pam Stacey, Co-Producer and writer of the film *America's Underwater Treasures*; Don Santee, Chief of Expeditions, and Holly Lohuis, Expedition Biologist for reviewing and fact checking the manuscript
- All of the members of the *America's Underwater Treasures* expedition team for sharing their stories and allowing us to explore the sanctuaries through their eyes
- Dr. Sylvia Earle for her Foreword
- Fabien and Céline Cousteau
- Dr. Jane Lubchenco, Administrator, National Oceanic and Atmospheric Administration
- Daniel Basta, Director, National Marine Sanctuary System, NOAA

- Matt Stout, Communications Director, National Oceanic and Atmospheric Administration
- Sarah Marquis, West Coast/Pacific Media Coordinator, National Marine Sanctuary System, NOAA
- William Douros, Regional Director, West Coast Region, National Marine Sanctuaries
- National Marine Sanctuary Superintendents, especially Chris Mobley (Channel Islands), Paul Michel Monterey Bay), Maria Brown (Farallones), Dan Howard (Cordell Bank), and Carol Bernthal (Olympic Coast)
- National Marine Sanctuary Staff and Volunteers
- National Marine Sanctuary Foundation, Jason Patlis, President, and Lori Arguelles, Past-President
- Dr. Maia McGuire, Research Editor and Compiler
- Nate Myers, Cover Designs and Interior Layouts

- And a special "Thank You" to Carrie Vonderhaar from the Ocean Publishing Team for her incredible assistance and coordination. She is absolutely terrific!

Glossary

Abiotic: of or characterized by the absence of life or living organisms.

Abyss: a deep, immeasurable space, gulf, or cavity; vast chasm

Algae: any of numerous groups of chlorophyll-containing, mainly aquatic organisms ranging from microscopic single-celled forms to multicellular forms 100 feet (30 meters) or more long. Algae are distinguished from plants by the absence of true roots, stems and leaves and by a lack of nonreproductive cells in the reproductive structures.

Algin: any hydrophilic, colloidal substance found in or obtained from various kelps.

Anadromous: (of fish) migrating from salt water to spawn in fresh water.

Anthropogenic: caused or produced by humans.

Ballast water: water carried temporarily in a vessel to provide desired draft and stability

Bedform: a depositional feature on the bed of a river or other body of flowing water that is formed by the movement of the bed material due to the flow.

Benthic: of or pertaining to the biogeographic region that includes the bottom of a lake, sea, or ocean.

Biotic: pertaining to life

Cephalopod: any mollusk of the class Cephalopoda, having tentacles attached to the head, including the cuttlefish, squid and octopus.

Cetacean: belonging to the Cetacea, an order of aquatic, chiefly marine mammals, including the whales and dolphins; a cetacean mammal

Crinoid: any echinoderm of the class Crinoidea, having a cup-shaped body to which are attached branched, radiating arms, comprising the sea lilies, feather stars, and various fossil forms.

Demersal: living or found near or in the deepest part of a body of water.

Desiccation: removing most of the water from (a substance of material); becoming dried up.

El Niño: a warm ocean current of variable intensity that develops after late December along the coast of Ecuador and Peru and sometimes causes catastrophic weather conditions.

Estuary/estuarine: that part of the mouth or lower course of a river in which the river's current meets the sea's tide; an arm or inlet of the sea at the lower end of a river.

Fauna: the animals of a given region or period considered as a whole

Fluorescence: the emission of radiation, especially of visible light, by a substance during exposure to external radiation such as light.

Genetic bottleneck: an evolutionary event in which a significant percentage of a population or species is killed or otherwise prevented from reproducing. A slightly different sort of genetic bottleneck can occur if a small group becomes reproductively separated from the main population.

Heterogeneity: composition from dissimilar parts; disparateness.

Hydrographer: a scientist who measures, describes and maps the surface waters of the earth, with special reference to their use for navigation.

Indigenous: originating in and characteristic of a particular region or country; native.

Invasive: non-native plants or animals that have a negative environmental, economic or social impact.

Invertebrate: an animal without a backbone.

Keystone species: a species that plays a critical role in maintaining the structure of an ecological community and whose impact on the community is greater than would be expected based on its relative abundance or total biomass.

La Niña: a cooling of the surface water of the eastern and central Pacific Ocean, occurring somewhat less frequently than El Niño events, but causing similar, generally opposite distruptions to global weather patterns.

Macroalgae: macroscopic, multicellular benthic marine algae, often called seaweed.

Midden: a mound consisting of shells of edible mollusks and other refuse, marking the site of a prehistoric human habitation

Nudibranch: a shell-less, marine snail of the suborder Nudibranchia, having external, often branched respiratory appendages on the back and sides.

Oophagy: literally "egg eating"; the practice of embryos feeding on eggs produced by the ovary while still inside the mother's uterus

Pelagic: of or pertaining to the open seas or oceans; living or growing at or near the surface of the ocean, far from land

Phytoplankton: the aggregate of plants and plantlike organisms in plankton.

Pinniped: an animal belonging to the Pinnepedia, a suborder of carnivores with limbs adapted to an aquatic life, including the seals and walruses.

Planktonic: the aggregate of passively floating, drifting or somewhat motile organisms occurring in a body of water, primarily comprising microscopic algae and protozoa.

Pod: a small herd or school, especially of seals or whales.

Polychaete: any marine annelid worm of the class Polychaeta, having a distinct hear and paired fleshy appendages that bear bristles and are used in swimming.

Productivity: in a biological sense, the rate at which organic matter is produced.

Rookery: a breeding place or colony of gregarious birds or animals, as penguins or seals.

Sea stack: a geological landform consisting of a steep and often vertical column or columns of rock in the sea near a coast, isolated by erosion

Sedentary: abiding in one place; not migratory

Sessile: permanently attached; not freely moving

Sentinel: being an individual or part of a population potentially susceptible to an infection or infestation that is being monitored for the appearance or recurrence of the causative pathogen or parasite.

Substrate: the base or material on which a nonmotile organism lives or grows

Transient: not lasting, enduring or permanent; transitory; staying only a short time.

Trophic level: any of the sequential stages in a food chain.

Turbidity: a measure of how clear or cloudy water is

Umbilical cable: a cable which supplies required consumables (e.g. power) to an apparatus such as an ROV (remotely-operated vehicle.)

Upwelling: the process by which warm, less-dense surface water is drawn away from along a shore by offshore currents and replaced by cold, denser water brought up from the sub-surface

Watershed: the region or area drained by a river, stream, etc.; drainage area

Zooplankton: the aggregate of animal or animal-like organisms in plankton

Index

Biographies

Jean-Michel Cousteau

Explorer. Environmentalist. Educator. Film Producer. For half a century, Jean-Michel Cousteau has dedicated himself and his vast experience to communicate to people of all nations and generations his love and concern for our water planet.

Since first being "thrown overboard" by his father at the age of seven with newly invented SCUBA gear on his back, Jean-Michel has been exploring the ocean realm. The son of ocean explorer Jacques Cousteau, Jean-Michel has investigated the world's oceans aboard *Calypso* and *Alcyone* for much of his life. Honoring his heritage, Jean-Michel founded Ocean Futures Society in 1999 to carry on this pioneering work.

Ocean Futures Society, a non-profit marine conservation and education organization, serves as a "Voice for the Ocean" by communicating in all media the critical bond between people and the sea and the importance of wise environmental policy. As Ocean Future's spokesman, Jean-Michel serves as an impassioned diplomat for the environment, reaching out to the public through a variety of media.

Jean-Michel has received many awards, including the Emmy, the Peabody Award, the 7 d'Or, and the Cable Ace Award, and has produced over 80 films. Cousteau is the executive producer of the highly acclaimed PBS television *series Jean-Michel Cousteau: Ocean Adventures*. In 2006, more than three million Americans learned about the sanctuaries for the first time from the award-winning film *America's Underwater Treasures*, part of the *Ocean Adventures* series. Also in 2006, Jean-Michel's initiative to protect the Northwest Hawaiian Islands took him to The White House where he screened, *Voyage to Kure*, for President George W. Bush. The President was inspired and in June 2006, he declared the 1,200-mile chain of islands a Marine National Monument—at the time; the largest marine protected area in the world.

Jean-Michel is also one of the founders of the National Marine Sanctuary Foundation and is currently a Trustee Emeritus.

Most recently, Jean-Michel and his Ocean Futures Society team were among the first to survey and film under water at the Gulf of Mexico Deep Horizon oil spill. Their footage was used as evidence that large masses of oil and dispersant were traveling under water.

The mission of Ocean Futures Society is to explore our global ocean, inspiring and educating people throughout the world to act responsibly for its protection, documenting the critical connection between humanity and nature, and celebrating the ocean's vital importance to the survival of all life on our planet.

"Protect the ocean and you protect yourself"

Ocean Futures Society is a non-profit 501(c) (3) organization, U.S. tax ID #95-4455199

Dr. Sylvia A. Earle

Dr. Sylvia A. Earle is a longtime friend of Jean-Michel Cousteau and has been a member of the Ocean Futures Society Advisory Board since its beginning in 1999. She is a pioneer in ocean exploration and research and is currently an Explorer-in-Residence at the National Geographic Society, leader of the Sustainable Seas Expeditions, chair of the Advisory Councils for Harte Research Institute and for the Ocean in Google Earth. Dr. Earle also served as Chief Scientist of NOAA in the early 1990s and she is a 2009 recipient of the coveted TED Prize for her proposal to establish a global network of Marine Protected Areas. Dr. Earle is one of the founders of the National Marine Sanctuary Foundation and is currently a Trustee Emeritus.

Dr. Maia McGuire

Dr. Maia McGuire, Research Editor and Compiler for this book, has been the University of Florida Sea Grant Extension Agent for northeast Florida since 2001. She holds a BS in Marine Biology and a PhD in Marine Biology and Fisheries. Prior related experience was with Harbor Branch Oceanographic Institution. Dr. McGuire is an active member in several organizations, including the National Marine Educators Association, Florida Marine Science Education Association, and the Association of Natural Resource Education Professionals, among others. She has won several honors and frequently speaks at regional and national conferences.

Jean-Michel Cousteau: Photo credit: Carrie Vonderhaar, Ocean Futures Society
Dr. Sylvia Earle: Photo credit: Carrie Vonderhaar, Ocean Futures Society
Dr. Maia McGuire: Photo credit: Debbi Penrose, Florida School for the Deaf and the Blind

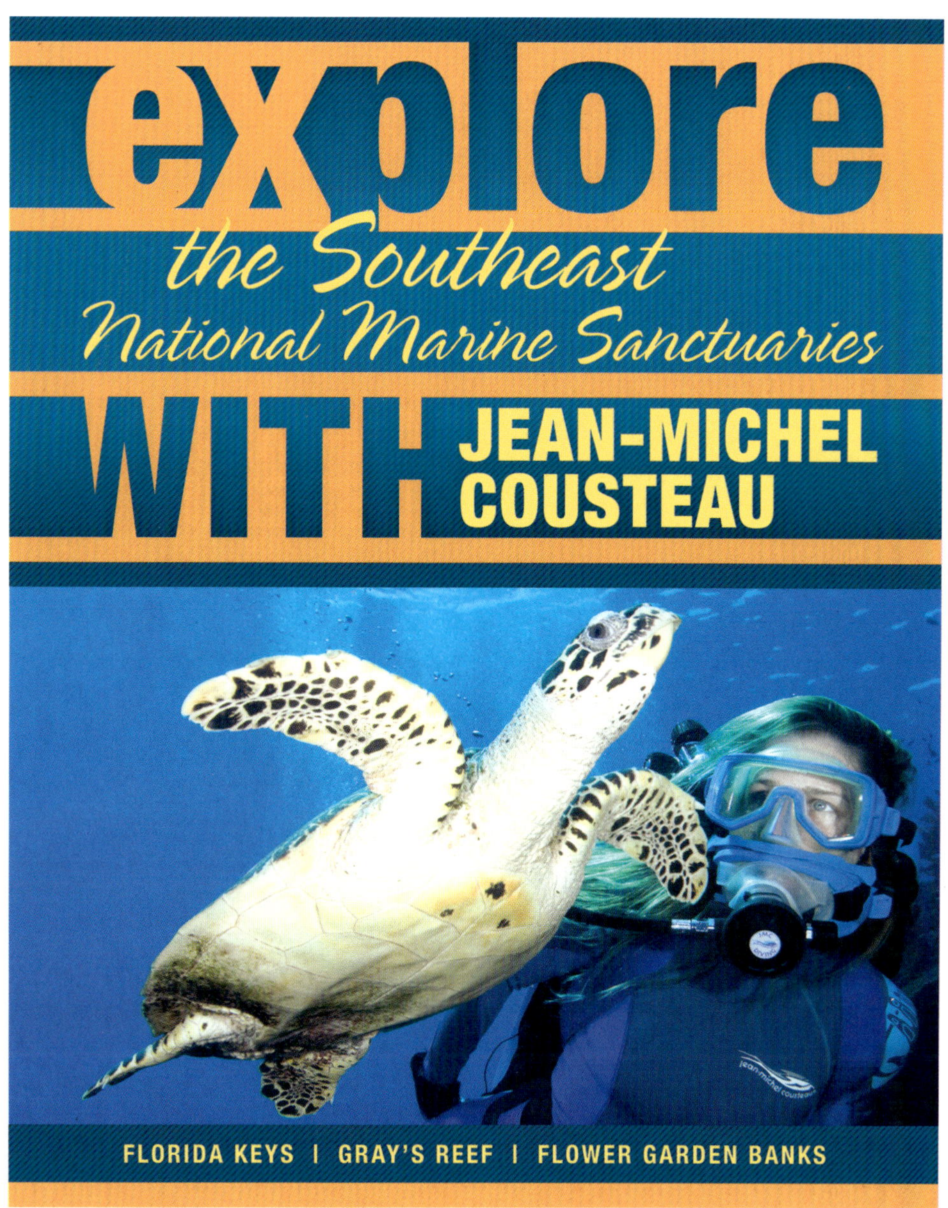

Available at all booksellers

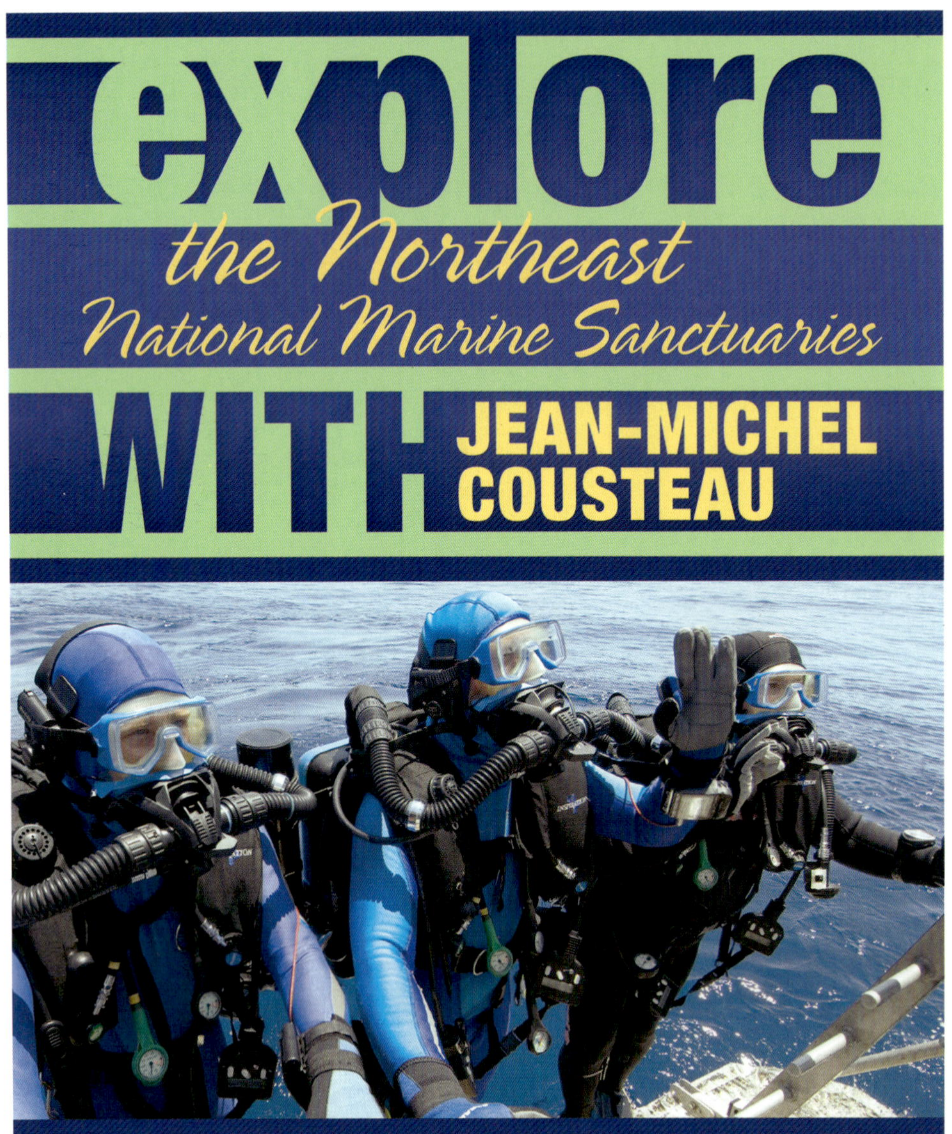

Available Spring 2012

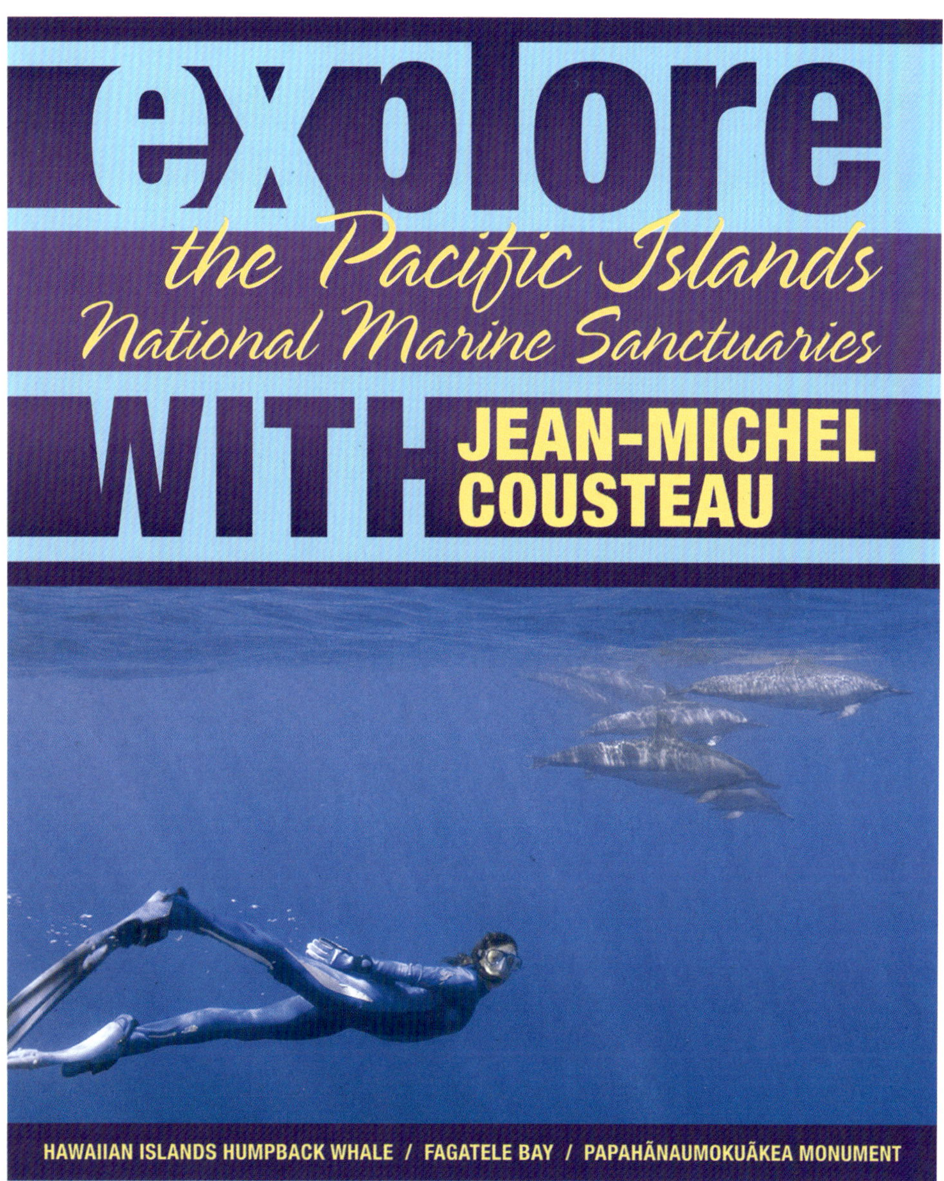

Available Fall 2012